Does God
Approve of War?

Does God Approve of War?

Christopher Brearley

Sovereign World

Sovereign World Ltd
PO Box 784
Ellel
Lancaster LA1 9DA
England

ISBN 978–1–85240–466–6

Cover design by Terry Dugan Design Group
Typeset by CRB Associates, Reepham, Norfolk
Printed in Malta

Contents

Introduction

The vast majority of people would agree that war is rarely a good option and that it can be justified only as a tragic last resort, if at all. It separates and destroys families and friends. Hearts are filled with hatred instead of love for our neighbors, and irreparable damage is done to the face of this beautiful world. Yet despite these stark truths, humanity's insatiable appetite for aggression continues undiminished. Why should this be? Obviously the root of the problem is not the weapon but the one who builds it. During a lecture delivered in 1948 the physicist Albert Einstein, whose theories of relativity revolutionized man's attitude about the nature of time and space, made the following comment relating to the threat of nuclear warfare: "It is not a physical problem, but an ethical one. What terrifies us is not the explosive force of the atomic bomb, but the power of the wickedness of the human heart, its explosive power for evil."

The above statement echoes what the Bible teaches. David asks God to rescue him from "men of violence, who devise evil plans in their hearts and stir up war every day" (Psalm 140:1–2). Jesus makes it abundantly clear that "out of men's hearts, come evil thoughts, sexual immorality, theft, murder, adultery, greed, malice, deceit, lewdness, envy, slander, arrogance and folly" (Mark 7:20–22). To alienate oneself from God will inevitably lead to disorder and evil practice that result in fights and quarrels.

How should a Christian react to war? "There is a time to kill and a time to heal . . . a time for war and a time for peace," said the Teacher (Ecclesiastes 3:3, 8). Does this condone war at certain times? Is it possible to have peace where there is injustice? Why does God allow war? "Why?" and "How?" are questions so useful that they cannot be asked too often! A Cameroonian proverb says, "He who asks questions cannot avoid answers." This is sound teaching, for difficult questions often need to be asked when searching for the truth.

I have made no attempt to escape the controversy associated with this topic. Nor have I sought it for its own sake, or claim to have a monopoly on the truth. My only aim is for a constructive, conscientious and considerate analysis. To achieve this it is essential to approach the subject with an open mind and an open Bible. Blessed are the rational. Although an uncanonical beatitude I trust that it would describe this book and its author.

Anyone who seriously studies the subject of "Does God Approve of War?" is confronted with many questions which do not have a simple yes or no answer. There is a bewildering array of opinions from which to choose that can leave you exhausted and confused at the end of your study. Undoubtedly in the short account which follows there will be some notable omissions, but I hope and pray that it will help to clarify the situation through honest debate and not create further problems. If so, my efforts will have been well rewarded.

Christopher Brearley

Setting the Scene

About seventeen kilometers north-west of Munich is Dachau. Each year it attracts many visitors who come not to see the picturesque town, but the site of Germany's first concentration camp. Today little remains of the original buildings, though a permanent exhibition of heart-rending photographs accompanied by text in several languages speaks for itself. Pictures depicting large piles of emaciated dead bodies awaiting the crematoria leave an indelible impression upon almost all who visit. It is extremely difficult, and for some impossible, to comprehend the vast scale of suffering and the horrific brutality.

Even so, it was far from being the most deadly of the camps. For example, Treblinka in German-occupied Poland was the location of a camp that existed for the sole purpose of extermination. It was a death factory, and the total number killed by gassing is estimated to be between 700,000 and 900,000 during the camp's seventeen months of operation. An average of over 10,000 a week, and this was just one camp.

The largest and most notorious extermination camp built by the Nazis was undoubtedly Auschwitz, also in Poland. It consisted of three camps: Auschwitz I, built in 1940; Auschwitz II, or Birkenau, built in 1941; and Auschwitz III, or

Monowitz, built in 1942. Although most visitors see only the main Auschwitz section of the complex it was at Birkenau, about three kilometers away, that the vast majority of the killing occurred. It is estimated that over one million died here, of whom around 85 per cent were Jews, along with Romanies, Poles and other European nationalities, before the Soviet Army liberated the camp in May 1945.

Up to two thousand people at a time could be killed within fifteen to twenty minutes using Zyklon B cyanide gas; their naked corpses were then burnt in open pits or incinerated in the crematoria. A minority who escaped death were condemned to slave labor, torture, disease, mass starvation and medical experimentation.

During World War II, Nazi Germany and its collaborators were responsible for the extermination of approximately six million Jewish men, women and children, because of the fanatic and foolish belief that they were carriers of genetic inheritance that mortally threatened German and Christian values. Ethnic violence has frequently occurred in world history, but this attempt by a modern government to exterminate an entire people is unique. The question "How can you believe in a God who permits suffering on this scale?" was undoubtedly asked. It would be wrong if it weren't.

On one of the spurs of Mount Herzl, in Jerusalem, marked from afar by a tall iron pillar, stands Israel's national Holocaust memorial and museum, Yad Va-Shem. This ensures that the Jews who died at the hands of the Nazis are not forgotten and pleads: "never again"; but action is much harder. The Hebrew words *yad va-shem* – hand (or monument) and name – are taken from the prophet Isaiah,

> "... I will give within my temple and its walls
>   a memorial and a name

better than sons and daughters;
   I will give them an everlasting name
      that will not be cut off."

(Isaiah 56:5)

Despite Germany's desire to annihilate them the nation lives on, but where was the God of Abraham, Isaac and Jacob in their time of desperate need?

The two World Wars of the twentieth century resulted in many millions of deaths and untold physical and psychological suffering on all sides. Prime Minister Neville Chamberlain, in a speech at Kettering on 3 July 1938, said, "In war, whichever side may call itself the victor, there are no winners, but all are losers." This is an important fact to be remembered, but unfortunately people today make the same mistakes as those of previous generations.

History Repeats Itself

The Bible records numerous wars in which God's people were involved and still today nations which bear the name of Christian are implicated in many conflicts. Christians are confronted daily with difficult questions that need to be answered. For instance, should the decision of the US and its allies to go to war with Iraq in March 2003 be condoned or condemned? The only certainty would appear to be that opinions are divided regardless of one's political or religious beliefs. Some would accuse President George W. Bush and Prime Minister Tony Blair of being warmongers, whilst others would praise them for their courageous decisions.

It could be argued that the intelligence information relating to the possession by Iraq of biological and chemical weapons of mass destruction, and the primary reason used to justify the war, was unreliable. The chief US investigator, Charles Dueffler, discovered that stockpiles of such weapons did not exist at the time of the US-led invasion. Hence, this would suggest that war was unjustified. Alternatively it could be said that it was essential to remove Iraqi leader Saddam Hussein and a brutal regime that tortured and murdered thousands of their own innocent citizens. There are many arguments for and against this war. Did the removal from power of the Iraqi leadership make the world a safer place; or has it helped to create an increase in worldwide terrorism?

Terrorism

On Tuesday September 11, 2001 the course of history was changed. Terrorists hijacked two commercial airplanes and crashed them into the two 110-storey towers of the World Trade Center complex in New York City. Within an hour, another hijacked plane crashed into the Pentagon, the nation's military headquarters near Washington, DC, and, shortly after that, a fourth hijacked airplane crashed into a rural area in Somerset County, Pennsylvania. These crashes destroyed the twin towers along with some neighboring buildings and a large proportion of one side of the Pentagon, and several thousand people were killed. This was the deadliest suicide terrorist attack to date and provoked reactions of sorrow, anger and disbelief. In a televised speech that evening, President Bush said, "Today our country saw evil." Why did God allow this atrocity to happen?

After concentrating on the Soviet Union for many years, the CIA, the British Military Intelligence Agencies and others have now realized that fundamentalist religious groups are probably the major threat to civilization in the twenty-first century. Al Qa'eda, meaning "The Base" in Arabic, was founded by the Saudi-born Osama bin Laden in Afghanistan during 1988. One of many Anti-American organizations, it supports the universal activities of Muslim extremists and so threatens the security of everyone. Car bombings, suicide bombings, hijackings, the release of harmful substances, cyber terrorism, and hostage-taking that often results in brutal murder are a feature of life, and the situation can only get worse. This is because of increased mobility, the Internet and the greater lethality of biological, chemical or nuclear weapons.

The fact that terrorists are also dependent upon publicity to achieve their objectives means that it is necessary for them to engage in increasing levels of depravity and high-profile attacks. A terrorist's aim is primarily not to maim or kill, but rather to destroy democracy and freedom by creating instability, alarm and psychological casualties amongst a worldwide audience. Anzwar Aziz, an Islamic Jihad member who blew himself up in an ambulance in Gaza, in December 1993, had frequently told friends: "Battles for Islam are won not through the gun but by striking fear into the enemy's heart." Hence, the targets chosen are often locations such as churches, mosques, synagogues, temples, hospitals and schools, where the maximum number of people can be impacted, and particularly the most vulnerable members of society. The greater the shock value, the greater the media coverage.

Not only Russians but people everywhere were shocked when pro-Chechen terrorists captured a school at Beslan in September 2004. The massacre which followed resulted in the death of more than 330 adults and children. Undoubtedly family and friends had prayed fervently for a peaceful solution. Why didn't God help them in their time of utter helplessness? If God is good, why is there so much wickedness?

There Is Nothing New under the Sun

In times of war and suffering, where is God? This question was repeatedly asked in the Bible. The psalmists, Elijah, Habakkuk, Jeremiah, Job and others found the apparent triumph of evil difficult to comprehend.

> How long, O LORD? Will you forget me for ever?
>   How long will you hide your face from me?
> How long must I wrestle with my thoughts
>   and every day have sorrow in my heart?
>   How long will my enemy triumph over me?
>
> (Psalm 13:1–2)

> Why do you hide your face
>   and forget our misery and oppression?
>
> (Psalm 44:24)

> Your eyes are too pure to look on evil;
>   you cannot tolerate wrong.
> Why then do you tolerate the treacherous?
>   Why are you silent while the wicked
>   swallow up those more righteous than themselves?
>
> (Habakkuk 1:13)

> You are always righteous, O LORD,
>   when I bring a case before you.
> Yet I would speak with you about your justice:
>   Why does the way of the wicked prosper?
>   Why do all the faithless live at ease?
>
> (Jeremiah 12:1)

> "Why do the wicked live on,
>   growing old and increasing in power?"
>
> (Job 21:7)

The questions raised in such verses cause perplexity for numerous Christians. How can wickedness be harmonized with God's absolute holiness? How should Christians react to the seeming injustice within the world today?

Pacifism or War?

My aim in what follows is not to provide a quick answer to the extremely difficult theological questions relating to war. Nor is it my desire to question the existence, the love or the absolute sovereignty of God. Rather it is an attempt to create a firm foundation upon which one can build a reasoned debate so as to try and attain satisfactory conclusions.

There are many who believe that Christians should actively be speaking out against war. Is that a responsible attitude in that it is more likely to lead to peace in the future? Or is it irresponsible because it will only lead to greater problems? President Theodore Roosevelt, in a speech at the Sorbonne on 23 April 1910, said, "War is a dreadful thing, and unjust war is a crime against humanity. But it is such a crime because it is unjust, not because it is war." Would you agree with that statement? Can war ever be justified? Should lethal force ever be used to resist evil? Was it right to wage war to defend the Jews from extermination by Hitler and his evil regime? Was the German Lutheran pastor, theologian and former pacifist Dietrich Bonhoeffer justified in supporting the attempted assassination of Hitler? Many Christians would consider it to be wrong to resist evil with violence, whilst others would unequivocally support such action.

Some people will accept that every war must be judged individually. They believe that a war must be morally justified; if not, then it should not be fought. There are times when a non-pacifist will consider a war to be immoral and so feel unable to be a part of it. Unprovoked aggression would be a possible example of this. Alternatively there are situations where extreme wickedness occurs and innocent men, women and children are persecuted. Should there then, and only then, be a righteous act of restraint on that evil to remove it?

The tradition of "just war" theory has aimed at recognizing those circumstances which make it morally legitimate to wage war. It was developed initially by the Christian Church, the most systematic exposition being that of Saint Thomas Aquinas. In his *Summa Theologicae* he provides the general outline of what became the just war theory.

Today, international law examines war primarily from two angles. First, it considers the legitimate reasons for going to war and, second, it regulates how wars are fought. *Jus ad bellum* (justice in going to war) is the title given to the branch of law that examines the criteria determining when the use of violence is justifiable. *Jus in bello* (justice in the conduct of war) by contrast, is the set of laws that come into effect once a war has begun. They serve as guidelines to regulate how combatants are to act.

Jus ad bellum says that a war is just only if:

1. It is authorized by legitimate authority. This excludes private individuals: only governments can initiate war.
2. There is a just cause. For example, self-defense against an armed attack to redress an injury is always considered to be a just cause, whilst material gain is not. Obviously if this rule were universally observed, all aggression and war would cease. It is, of course, often difficult to define what is meant by "defense." Pre-emptive strikes can be legitimate in some circumstances in order to prevent injustice before it occurs.
3. It is motivated by a good or right intention in order to secure a just and lasting peace for friend and foe alike.

4. The violence used is proportionate to the offense of provocation. Opposing forces should never be subject to greater punishment than is necessary to secure victory and peace. This principle overlaps into the moral guidelines of how a war should be conducted, namely the principles of *jus in bello*.

5. There is a reasonable probability of success. Any suffering incurred fighting for a lost cause is not morally justifiable.

6. It is the last resort. Every conceivable non-violent option such as diplomacy and economic pressure must be reasonably exhausted before the use of force can be justified.

In the conduct of war (*jus in bello*), both political and military authorities must observe the two principles of:

1. *proportionality*: the amount of violence used must never on any occasion exceed what is necessary to achieve victory, thus avoiding unnecessary death and destruction. Neither must the act of war be greater than its expected good consequences;

2. *discrimination*: just warfare must discriminate between combatants and civilians. Force in acts of war must be directed against legitimate targets. Therefore, this would prohibit the bombing of civilian residential areas where there is no military presence. Civilians are not permissible targets of war and every effort must be taken to avoid killing them.

Together these two principles provide useful guidelines. However, they do invoke a plethora of problems in that their vagueness often leads to differing interpretations.

Many who accept a just-war position would oppose the use of biological, chemical or nuclear weapons because of the often widespread, indiscriminate and uncontrollable effects that may continue long after conflict has ceased. Others are of the opinion that war and violence, of any description, is morally unjustified and that all disputes can be settled by peaceful means. They might argue that God the Father is "the God of peace" (1 Thessalonians 5:23), God the Son is the "Prince of Peace" (Isaiah 9:6), and the Holy Spirit is likened to a dove (Matthew 3:16), a bird considered to be a symbol of peace.

Jesus is frequently regarded and portrayed as a pacifist. The Christian is told to love not only his neighbors, but also his enemies (Matthew 5:44). Therefore, does the teaching of Jesus in the Sermon on the Mount forbid a Christian from being a member of the armed forces? May a Christian engineer or research scientist be involved in military work? May a Christian be a member of the police force if it involves the use of weapons to maintain law and order? What is the Christian's duty in today's complicated world? These are questions which are not easily resolved for they refer to areas in which there is no clear overall consensus. Some groups will support defensive but not offensive war, whilst others oppose all war, but believe in maintaining a police force; absolute pacifists believe that any form of coercive or disciplinary force is unacceptable and counterproductive.

Understandably one yearns for a time when there will be undisturbed tranquility within the world. However, it must be accepted that wars and rumors of wars are part of the present world order. Man by himself can never achieve lasting political peace and so Christians must live and suffer in an evil world (Mark 13:7–8). Christians are in a battle, physical and spiritual, and will be so with increasing intensity until Christ returns. Meanwhile, what is God's attitude to war? Do pacifist groups generally appear to be stronger in conviction and emotional commitment than on theological foundations? To answer these questions there is only one reliable source – the complete Bible.

Summary

People do understand that horrible things happen in war. Yet despite this awful truth, war continues unabated from one generation to the next. It would appear that the situation can only get worse, primarily because of ever-increasing terrorism and the continual development of more lethal military technology. Throughout history Christians have been challenged about how they should react toward war and have conscientiously disagreed. Some adopt a position of absolute pacifism which they claim to base upon the teaching of Jesus and refuse to destroy human life under any circumstances. As a result they could be accused of failing to oppose tyranny, thereby preventing the establishment of justice. Was Jesus really a pacifist? Others will support war and violence if they believe that it can be morally justified. However, evaluating the "justness" of a war can be extremely difficult. What sort of war is just? For example, is it possible to justify the use of nuclear weapons, or anything that causes indiscriminate death and destruction? Surely in modern warfare it is virtually impossible to target military forces and installations without attacking densely populated areas and so inevitably there will be many civilian casualties. Are there any major wars in history where civilians have not suffered? Hence, should one conclude that no war can be "just"? Whatever our views it is always healthy to examine them constantly in the light of Scripture.

To think about and discuss

1. If God is just, why does He continue to allow injustice to prevail?
2. How can you believe in a God who permits suffering on a vast scale?
3. Several hundred were killed at Beslan despite much fervent prayer for a peaceful solution. What would you say to the bereaved?
4. Are there criteria that clearly ascertain what is a justifiable, and what is not a justifiable war?

A Rational View

People in the public eye are often quoted out of context. Journalists in search of sensationalism will not hesitate to overemphasize or minimize important points and so often report the opposite to that which was clearly intended. Therefore, you should not believe everything that you are told without examination. Be like the Bereans who received the message with great eagerness and examined the Scriptures every day to see if what Paul said was true (Acts 17:11). They had a thorough and unprejudiced approach in their search for the truth which is always an admirable way of proceeding. Their attitude emphasizes that it is only when all the evidence is examined, that a judgment should be made.

The English jurist, scholar and orientalist John Selden rightly said, "We pick out a text here and there to make it serve our turn; whereas, if we take it all together, and considered what went before and what followed after, we should find it meant no such thing" ("The Scriptures," *Table Talk*, 1689). By taking verses of the Bible out of context it is possible to prove or disprove almost anything that you wish. For example, take the following two verses, one from the Old Testament and one from the New:

> Show no pity: life for life, eye for eye, tooth for tooth, hand for hand, foot for foot.
>
> (Deuteronomy 19:21; cf. Exodus 21:24–25; Leviticus 24:20)

> "Do not suppose that I have come to bring peace to the earth. I did not come to bring peace, but a sword."
>
> (spoken by Jesus, Matthew 10:34)

Can they be used to advocate the need for retaliation whenever a person is wronged? Are such verses an obvious justification for war?

In order to argue their case, pacifists might choose such verses as:

> "Do not seek revenge or bear a grudge against one of your people, but love your neighbor as yourself . . . "
>
> (Leviticus 19:18)

And undoubtedly would quote the sixth commandment,

> "You shall not murder."
>
> (Exodus 20:13)

The teaching of Jesus was,

> "You have heard that it was said, 'Eye for eye, and tooth for tooth.' But I tell you, Do not resist an evil person. If someone strikes you on the right cheek, turn to him the other also."
>
> (Matthew 5:38–39)

Do these words of Jesus suggest that the New Testament replaces the Old Testament?

The entire Bible is God's Word and so it is not negotiable.

Having said that, how does one tackle the apparent discrepancies? Can apparently opposing statements both be correct? One simple explanation can be provided by comparing proverbs, many of ancient origin, which occur in everyday language. These usually contain wise advice which should be heeded and practiced, for if you only quote them they are of no benefit. However, there are those who would question the value of proverbs and say that for almost every known proverb, you can find one that says exactly the opposite. For instance, if "money isn't everything," can it also be true that "money makes the world go round?" Would it not be logical to assume that two contradictory proverbs cannot both be true? Doesn't the contradiction cancel their value? Or does it convey a message about the nature of reality? Life is contradictory and so some proverbs may only be applicable to certain circumstances. Hence, "circumstances alter cases" becomes a key proverb. Different action may be necessitated by changed circumstances and therefore, "One man's meat is another man's poison."

When reading the Bible it is important to have an overall perspective of the situation prior to analyzing the detail. You need to be familiar with the circumstances: not only what God said, but why He said it. Without this approach it is easy to misinterpret His Word and so become confused and discouraged by difficulties. Also it is an essential rule of interpretation that no passage of Scripture should be interpreted in a way that contradicts the overall message of the Bible. What may appear to be discrepancies are not. For example, the Bible repeatedly states that God is a God of love and this is not a fluctuating emotion but a constant characteristic. How then can God ever permit the ravages of war? Are the love and the law of God irreconcilable opposites? The answer is, definitely not. By faith one must accept that God is holy and intolerant of sin. He always acts in love. There is no alternative to this fundamental truth.

Militant Reactionaries

Sadly, truth is often distorted to create a religious ideology that incites hatred. This is well illustrated by the Jewish Zealots who were very active in the Galilean area of Palestine during the first century AD. They formed an antimonarchist party and were intolerant of anyone who threatened their partisan perspective. Accordingly extremists amongst them turned to terrorism and assassination. They became known as "Sicarii" (Greek *sikarioi*, "dagger men") because of their practice of carrying daggers in order to murder those, including Jews, who sought peace and conciliation with pagan Rome, as they went about their everyday business. Zeal led to hatred in their aim to create a world Jewish theocracy. Charles Caleb Colton wisely said, "Whenever we find ourselves more inclined to persecute than to persuade, we may then be certain that our zeal has more of pride in it than of charity" (*Lacon* [1825], 1.17).

Some of the Jewish people initially thought that Jesus was a Zealot liberator who would lead them in rebellion against the constitutional government. However, when they realized that Jesus was not going to overthrow the political situation and solve their problems, they rejected Him. Encouraged by their priests they made false accusations against Him and demanded that He be executed (Matthew 27:20). Because of the Jews He was crucified on a Roman cross, though it must be acknowledged that others were also responsible (Acts 4:27). More importantly, we ourselves are also guilty because of our sins.

Stephen was stoned to death by Jews and,

> On that day a great persecution broke out against the church at Jerusalem, and all except the apostles were scattered throughout Judea and Samaria.
>
> (Acts 8:1)

It is true that, "Godly men buried Stephen and mourned deeply for him" (Acts 8:2), no doubt because they deplored the injustice of his death. In contrast the greatest ambition of Saul of Tarsus, prior to his conversion to Christianity, was to destroy the Church. He was blinded by prejudice and had blood on his hands (Acts 22:4; 26:10), for others followed Stephen into martyrdom.

Many atrocities have been committed in the name of Judaism, but the same could equally be said for Christianity. The Christian Crusades are a good illustration of this. In 1071 Jerusalem was ruled by the Seljuk Turks who did not welcome pilgrims from Europe. Consequently, Pope Urban II, at the Council of Claremont in 1095, instigated a crusade to liberate the Holy Places from Muslim domination. He promised remission of sins to all those who fought, and to all who died in the expedition immediate entry into Paradise. His listeners shouted, *"Deus vult"* (God wills it), which became the battle cry of the Crusaders. They captured the city for Christendom in 1099 and immediately massacred the Muslim inhabitants, including the women and children. This irresponsible and merciless fanaticism causes inflexibility within Islam even today.

Another example of brutality is the Inquisition, a name derived from the Latin verb *inquiro* ("inquire into"), which occurred in several parts of Europe and aimed to seek out those guilty of offences against Roman Catholic orthodoxy. At first, the use of torture to obtain confessions was rejected, but in 1252 it was authorized by Pope Innocent IV. Some suspects who refused to change their beliefs were sentenced to die by burning so as to purify the Church and prevent others following what were considered to be erroneous ways.

Mary, daughter of Henry VIII and Catherine of Aragon, who succeeded to the throne in July 1553, was a staunch Catholic and one of the most tragic of all English sovereigns. She showed great opposition to the Reformation movement and tried to re-impose the Roman Catholic faith on England. During her five-year reign several hundred Protestants suffered martyrdom, and thousands fled the country. "Bloody Mary" was well worthy of her title. Nor are Protestants innocent of having committed atrocities. It is an indisputable fact that many monstrous acts have been committed in the name of Christ – the Prince of Peace (Isaiah 9:6).

Understanding Islam

Today militant Islam poses a major threat to everyone regardless of their beliefs. The problem arises due to the interpretation of the key word *jihad*. Most people would consider it to mean a spiritual struggle, but militant Islam has a different understanding: "holy war." The vast majority of Muslims would accept that the Qur'an nowhere justifies terrorism such as that committed by Osama bin Laden and his followers. Consequently, since September 11, 2001 the governments of most Muslim states have openly opposed him. This is well illustrated by a front-page report in *Iran Today* (24 September 2001) which reads: "Iran has vehemently condemned the suicidal terrorist attacks in the United States and has expressed its deep sorrow and sympathy with the American nation." This is one example of the many public condemnations by Muslim states of terrorist atrocities.

Muslim extremists believe the opposite. They see their actions as a true *jihad* or holy war against the enemies of Islam. It is considered right and necessary to attack America, "the great Satan." She is regarded as an enemy of Allah (the Arabic term for God) because of her military attacks on Muslim people and, further, her complicity in the abuse of Palestinians by

Israel. Surely the American policy of arming and funding Israel was one of the main factors which provoked al-Qa'eda to plan and execute its 9/11 attacks.

On Sunday 9 October 2001 al-Jazeera satellite TV released a statement from Osama bin Laden. An excerpt referring to the attacks of September 11 says:

> America is filled with fear. America has been filled with horror from north to south and east to west, and thanks be to God what America is tasting now is only a copy of what we have tasted. God has blessed a group of vanguard Muslims to destroy America and may God bless them and allot them a supreme place in heaven.

Also in 2001, Osama bin Laden told ABC News producer Rahimullah Yousafsai that he would kill his own children if necessary, in order to hit American targets. Such language clearly represents his style and ideology.

Not only America but also her associates are prone to attack. Therefore, it should be no surprise that London suffered its first suicide bombings on 7 July 2005. Three attacks on underground trains and one on a bus near Tavistock Place resulted in the death of more than fifty innocent individuals and injured many more. One of the strongest early condemnations came from the Muslim Council of Britain. Following an emergency meeting, Sir Iqbal Sacranie, the Council's Secretary-General, said, "Nothing in Islam can ever justify the evil actions of the bombers. We are determined to work together with all concerned to prevent such an atrocity happening again." The Muslim Association of Britain through its spokesman Harris Bokhari said, "We cannot rule out the possibility of a conspiracy to carry out more attacks in the future, whether near or distant. An urgent measure would be to lend the police a helping hand in their investigations and their efforts to stem the threat altogether."

Despite widespread condemnation the terrorists would consider their actions to be justified by Islamic law. As with the Bible the Qur'an can be interpreted in a way that supports opposing opinions. An interpretation of *jihad* has been taken by Muslim terrorists to justify the legitimating of violence for achieving their aims. Namely: to force their version of Islam upon certain Muslim countries; establish a Palestinian state and destroy the State of Israel; and to be intolerant of anyone who dissents against their views.

The materials to make a human bomb are cheap and readily available and there is no shortage of martyrs. These bombers sincerely believe that what they are doing is not suicide, which is forbidden in Islam, but rather sacred explosions which are pleasing in the sight of Allah. An imam associated with Hamas – a militant Palestinian Islamic movement founded in 1987 – said, "The first drop of blood shed by a martyr during *jihad* washes away his sins instantaneously. On the Day of Judgment, he will face no reckoning. On the Day of Resurrection, he can intercede for seventy of his nearest and dearest to enter Heaven; and he will have at his disposal seventy-two *houris*, the beautiful maidens of Paradise." It should be stressed that this promised bliss is not sensual.

In all the above instances of religious extremism we have examples of evil being committed under the guise of good and in the name of God. It should always be remembered that earnestness, eagerness, enthusiasm and numerical strength are not necessarily signs that something is true (1 Kings 18:25–29). A proverb wisely reminds us that "mischief often begins in the name of the Lord." Unfortunately, even today, much evil is done with good intentions.

The Authority of the Bible

The following account accepts that the Bible is incapable of error because of its supernatural inspiration whereby God operated upon the minds of the writers (2 Peter 1:21). Therefore, the only thing that can be discussed is the interpretation, which raises an important question: How does one interpret the Bible? Much of the Bible is self-interpreting, and so the more you read it, the more you will find that a passage in one section explains a passage somewhere else. You cannot fully understand the New Testament if you haven't read the Old Testament, and vice versa. Certainly supporting materials such as a study Bible, commentaries, maps and especially an exhaustive concordance so as to locate related passages easily will be helpful. Most important of all it must be remembered that until your eyes are opened by the Holy Spirit, the Bible will be of no great help. Therefore, like the psalmist our prayer must be:

> Open my eyes that I may see
> wonderful things in your law.

(Psalm 119:18)

Then enjoy the search and may it end in the satisfaction which arises from keeping God's commandments. That is wisdom.

Summary

All of us are greatly influenced, probably more than we imagine, by our environment. Our decisions can easily be influenced by feelings instead of facts, thus leading to false conclusions that may be fatal. Within the Bible there are several references to false teachers who led people astray. They are likened to savage wolves who cause havoc (Acts 20:29–30).

In today's world truth is often intentionally distorted so as to promote a given cause and even incite intolerance or hatred. Propaganda is a common tool in times of war, either to dishearten the enemy psychologically or to portray them as an evil that needs to be fought. Sadly, many monstrous acts have been committed in the name of religion through a lack of discernment. People are indoctrinated to accept uncritically what are frequently partisan ideas. Young people are especially vulnerable to such teaching because they are generally more easily manipulated to accept the glorification of warfare and martyrdom. Terrorists, more often than not, sincerely believe that their atrocious deeds are pleasing in the sight of God. They fail to differentiate between right and wrong. Only the truth of the Bible revealed by the power of the Holy Spirit can make you wise.

To think about and discuss

1. "Things evidently false are not only printed, but many things of truth most falsely set forth" (Sir Thomas Browne, "To the Reader," *Religio Medici*, 1642). Do you agree with that statement? To what extent do the media influence society today?

2. Compare Deuteronomy 19:21 with Leviticus 19:18 and Matthew 5:38–39 with 10:34. Are these verses contradictory? If not, why not?

3. Does a Christian have a duty to help the state to defend its citizens or its territory if this involves the use of violence? What would I do if called on to participate in war?

4. Why do extremists preach intolerance and hatred to exploit and oppress others?

General Observations

For any research to be worthwhile it is necessary to observe all the facts without bias. Therefore, this chapter takes a panoramic view of the Bible, but makes no attempt to analyze the finer details. The only aim is to set the scene for further study so that decisions might be based upon Scripture rather than sentiment.

The Old Testament

The Book of Genesis is about beginnings. It explains the origin of the universe, the human race, sin, redemption; it also records the birth of Israel and how God promises Abram to make it into a great nation and give it the land of Canaan. Undoubtedly chapter 3 is one of the most important in all the Word of God because it is a foundation upon which several doctrines of faith are based. The fall of man explains many of our problems today, for when Adam sinned (v. 6), sin entered the entire human race (Romans 5:12), causing an ongoing tension and conflict. As a result of this, bloodshed occurred very early in the history of mankind. Cain attacked his brother Abel and killed him (Genesis 4:8). The same chapter (v. 23) refers to a man called Lamech, who boasts to his two wives about the violent shedding of blood. As far back as Noah's day, "the earth was corrupt in God's sight and was full of violence" (Genesis 6:11).

Exodus, often appropriately called the "Book of Redemption," is a sequel to Genesis. It details the deliverance of the Israelites from cruel bondage in Egypt, and the start of their journey through the Red Sea and the wilderness to the Promised Land. During this extremely long journey they encountered many serious difficulties. At Rephidim they were attacked by the Amalekites, whom by God's power they defeated (Exodus 17:8–15). Here (v. 9) is the first reference to Joshua, who became a key figure in Israel's history.

The account of Joshua describes the conquest of Canaan, its division amongst the tribes of Israel when the major military campaigns were completed, and the renewal of their covenant with God. War is a prominent feature because of the obstacles encountered in ousting their numerous enemies from the land. Hittites, Amorites, Perizzites, Jebusites and others all had to be conquered. Joshua's strategy reveals that he was a great military leader who faithfully and heroically performed the work which God had entrusted to him. Consequently, the tribes enjoyed unity and success, but following his death the situation rapidly deteriorated and lawlessness prevailed.

At this stage the first observation to be made in relation to God's attitude to war is that He sometimes told His people to fight and enabled them to win, even when they were greatly outnumbered. There are some who will find this objectionable, especially those occasions when the Israelites were commanded to exterminate a people, men and women, children and infants, and even their animals (see, e.g., Joshua 6:21; 1 Samuel 15:3).

The Book of Judges records Israel's history from the period of Joshua's death to the advent of the monarchy. This should have been a time of great blessing, but it was not because as a nation they refused to obey God. A key verse, written twice, says, "everyone did as he saw fit" (Judges 17:6; 21:25). Israel's leaders disobediently failed to remove the Canaanites from the land, which would result in harmful repercussions throughout the nation's life. This negligence caused many Israelites to sin by adopting Canaanite religious practices, forsaking the Lord and serving Baal and the Ashtoreths. Thus they violated the first commandment (Exodus 20:3), and accordingly experienced the disastrous consequences of the Lord's anger.

Therefore, the second observation is that God sometimes fought against His people. He punished their disobedience by delivering them into the hands of foreign oppressors such as the Mesopotamians, Moabites, Canaanites, Midianites, Ammonites and Philistines. Each time the Israelites sinned, they were punished by being invaded and then delivered by a judge raised up by God (Judges 2:16). Although Israel was frequently chastised by God, He never completely abandoned them.

During the period when Israel was governed by judges, anarchy prevailed, which resulted in the inauguration of the monarchy. The Books of Samuel record the political and religious life of the nation at this time and center around three principal characters: Samuel, the last of the judges, though primarily a prophet; Saul, the first king of Israel; and David, Israel's second and greatest king.

The request to Samuel for a king was tantamount to a rejection of God (1 Samuel 8:7). Discontent resulting in a desire for a change of leadership is a common characteristic of man in every generation, even though it may be for the worse. In this instance, Israel was again turning away from her Lord by rejecting His sovereignty. Despite this, the Lord granted Israel her request, but not without giving warning of the prerogatives of a king (1 Samuel 8:10–19). Saul, son of Kish, of the tribe of Benjamin, was anointed king and soon proved his worth with a decisive victory over Ammon. However, during his reign he was often rebellious toward God and although he admitted he had sinned (1 Samuel 15:30), his sorrow was doubtless false. Hence, he was rejected by God and his kingdom was transferred to David.

The defeat of the Philistine giant, Goliath, by David, justifiably gave him celebrity status. Sadly this made Saul jealous to such a degree that he spent years trying to kill David, but his attempts always failed. Though rejected by God, Saul continued to reign for many years but remained emotionally unstable. At the end of his life he was forced to face the Philistines in battle at Mount Gilboa. Here, Israel was ignominiously defeated and three of Saul's sons were killed. Saul himself was seriously wounded and, not wanting to be taken captive alive, committed suicide by falling on his own sword. Samuel's posthumous prophecy was fulfilled (1 Samuel 28:19) and the throne now awaited the accession of David, though it would be several years before he would rule all twelve tribes. David was accepted as king by Judah, but not the northern tribes who crowned Ish-Bosheth, another of Saul's sons. It was only following Ish-Bosheth's death that David was anointed king over all Israel (2 Samuel 5:1–5).

> And [David] became more and more powerful because the LORD God Almighty was with him.
>
> (2 Samuel 5:10)

Therefore, David was an able leader of men and allied to this was his outstanding success as a military man.

David desired to build a temple for God in Jerusalem but God told him that this was not within His will:

> "You are not to build a house for my Name, because you are a warrior and have shed blood."
>
> (1 Chronicles 28:3)

Undeniably David's numerous wars excluded him from build-
ing the temple. That is not to say that God disapproved of the
wars for He had blessed David and given him victory on various
occasions. The important issue is that God is a God of peace,
and this very essence of His nature was incompatible with
David, a man of war, being associated with the temple. One
day the temple would be built but by his son Solomon, whose
reign was a period of unprecedented peace and prosperity.
God was pleased that Solomon did not ask for the life of his
enemies (2 Chronicles 1:11). Although not a military man like
his father, he did take defensive measures, primarily the
fortification of key cities, thus guarding the main approaches
to the kingdom (1 Kings 9:15–19). Another major form of
defense was the war chariot. Solomon had a huge force
of chariots and horses.

Sadly in his latter years we are told that he was often foolish
and undiscerning:

> As Solomon grew old, his wives turned his heart after other
> gods, and his heart was not fully devoted to the LORD his God,
> as the heart of David his father had been. He followed
> Ashtoreth the goddess of the Sidonians, and Molech the
> detestable god of the Ammonites. So Solomon did evil in
> the eyes of the LORD; he did not follow the LORD completely,
> as David his father had done.
>
> (1 Kings 11:4–6)

However, if we consider that he was probably the author of
Ecclesiastes, it seems reasonable to conclude that he had a
correct relationship with God before he died. After wasting
much of his life he came to the conclusion that it was vital to
"[f]ear God and keep his commandments, for this is the whole
duty of man" (Ecclesiastes 12:13).

Towards the end of his reign, Solomon's kingdom experienced serious problems, both at home and abroad, which were the result of idolatry. The apostle Paul wrote, "Do not be deceived: God cannot be mocked. A man reaps what he sows" (Galatians 6:7). This law is applicable to all ages and Solomon's was no exception. His kingdom would be torn away from him and given to one of his subordinates. Mercifully this would not occur in his lifetime, but that of his son, and even then, for the sake of David, he would continue to rule one tribe (1 Kings 11:36).

The loss of revenues to Solomon from his reduced kingdom resulted in increased taxation for his people which naturally caused discontent. Therefore, following the death of Solomon the whole assembly of Israel requested that the new king, Rehoboam, reduce their heavy burden. Foolishly he refused to listen to the wise advice of the older men who had counseled his father. He paid no attention to the people's demands and so the northern tribes revolted and the kingdom was divided in two parts (1 Kings 12:1–15). Ten tribes kept the name of Israel and were ruled by Jeroboam, whilst the tribes of Judah and Benjamin formed the kingdom of Judah and continued to be ruled by the descendants of Solomon. Eventually both kingdoms would find themselves in captivity in foreign lands.

Rehoboam's immediate response to the division of his kingdom was to mobilize the armies of Judah and Benjamin and fight the army of Israel. But God spoke through Shemaiah to Rehoboam and all the people of Judah warning them against fighting their relations the Israelites, and so they did not attack. On this occasion God told them not to fight.

These divided and weakened kingdoms would inevitably fall for it was orchestrated by God. Following the capture of Samaria by Shalmaneser V in 722 BC, Israel ceased to exist as a sovereign power (2 Kings 17:3–6). Judah survived longer but fell to the Babylonians in 586 BC (2 Kings 25:1–21). However, it must be remembered that God had said to Abram,

> "All the land that you see I will give to you and your offspring forever."
>
> (Genesis 13:15)

This clearly indicates that the Israelites must one day return to Canaan for again it was all part of God's plan.

Prior to Judah being taken captive, Jeremiah had precisely prophesied that the period of exile would be seventy years (Jeremiah 25:11–21). This prophecy was fulfilled when the army of Cyrus, king of Persia, overthrew Babylon in 539 BC and liberated the Jews. A detailed picture of the "Restoration Period" can be gained by reading the books of Ezra, Nehemiah, Haggai, Zechariah and Malachi, whilst Esther is dated between chapters 6 and 7 of Ezra and provides a glimpse of life in Persia. It also reveals how the Jews escaped extermination by Haman and how his wicked plot recoiled on himself. Because the books of our English Old Testament are not grouped in chronological order, the history of Israel closes with the final chapter of Nehemiah (*c.* 425 BC).

The New Testament

Whereas the Old Testament speaks frequently about the participation by God's people in military action, the New Testament does not. On the surface, at least, the picture seems completely different. Repeatedly Jesus refused to fight when He could so easily have won. Neither did Jesus encourage His followers to use warfare as a means of conquest: He did the opposite. When Simon Peter attacked Malchus during His arrest (John 18:10), Jesus rebuked him saying:

"Put your sword back in its place ... for all who draw the sword will die by the sword. Do you think I cannot call on my Father, and he will at once put at my disposal more than twelve legions of angels? But how then would the Scriptures be fulfilled that say it must happen in this way?"

(Matthew 26:52–54)

Earlier in that monumental week Jesus had chosen to make His dramatic entry into Jerusalem on a donkey (Matthew 21:5), thus fulfilling the prophecy of Zechariah (Zechariah 9:9). Why did Jesus not ride on a horse of war? Why did He refuse to fight, allowing Himself instead to be led like a lamb to the slaughter? The answer is because of the purpose of His visit to earth. He came as the Prince of Peace (Isaiah 9:6). This is in stark contrast to His return when He will ride on a white horse in war (Revelation 19:11ff.). The first time He came not to condemn the world but to save it. The next time it will be to judge justly and wage war. Unfortunately the crowd missed the profound meaning of Jesus' choice of a donkey, and even the disciples who brought it to Him, only understood its significance after Jesus was glorified (John 12:16).

The fact that Jesus could raise Lazarus from the dead after being in a tomb for four days clearly demonstrated His extraordinary power. Surely He was the mighty deliverer who could liberate the Jews from Roman domination by leading a military uprising. Those who pinned their hope on a political deliverance were mistaken because Jesus did not come to establish an earthly kingdom. That is why He said to Pilate,

"My kingdom is not of this world. If it were, my servants would fight to prevent my arrest by the Jews. But now my kingdom is from another place."

(John 18:36)

It is impossible to establish a spiritual kingdom with physical force. Having said that, there are occasions where, during His time on earth, Jesus appears not to have been totally pacifistic. It cannot be ignored that Jesus did use physical force when He cleared the temple area:

> In the temple courts he found men selling cattle, sheep and doves, and others sitting at tables exchanging money. So he made a whip out of cords, and drove all from the temple area, both sheep and cattle; he scattered the coins of the money-changers and overturned their tables.
>
> (John 2:14–15)

What are we to understand by the word "all" in the above passage? Does it refer merely to the sheep and the cattle, as some pacifists would suggest? No, it includes also the buyers and the sellers who are engaged in a flagrant desecration of the temple courts. This view is well supported by Matthew 21:12. Jesus is burning with anger and indignation. Holy zeal for His father's house consumes Him. To claim that Jesus was a strict pacifist is nowhere more inaccurate than here. Clearly this was a violent physical response, and yet Jesus remained sinless. Even in this situation He did nothing wrong. Anger can be justified provided that it is not prolonged and does not lead to a lack of self-control (Ephesians 4:26). It is also not wrong to defend oneself. Jesus said to His disciples, "if you don't have a sword, sell your cloak and buy one" (Luke 22:36). When they traveled, it would have been necessary to carry a sword in order to fend off robbers. Jesus seems to be warning them to be prepared to defend themselves when necessary. Such an interpretation creates problems for many, especially in relation to Matthew 26:52, which some would claim condemns participation in war, even defensive war.

Looking again at Simon Peter's attack on the high priest's servant, it is clear that he was acting rashly without waiting for an answer to his question, "Lord, should we strike with our swords?" (Luke 22:49). His action was also unnecessary, for Jesus was not powerless. Had He desired, He could have prayed to His Father and instantly received the help of more than twelve legions of angels. Hence, Peter's efforts were foolish and futile. Although on this occasion Simon Peter acted inappropriately, Jesus' declaration that "all who draw the sword will die by the sword" should not be interpreted in a way that prohibits the use of the sword for defense of one's nation.

Paul writing to the Romans answers the question of how Christians should respond to evil-doers (Romans 12:14–21). He condemns persecution (v. 14), retaliation (v. 17) and a vengeful spirit (v. 19), and teaches that we are not to be overcome by evil, but are to overcome evil with good (v. 21). This echoes the words of Jesus in the Sermon on the Mount and is often quoted by those who adopt a Christian pacifist position.

Even so, in Romans 13 Paul asks for obedience to the governing authorities because they must resist evil, even with the sword. Does this justify war? Or are there exceptions to civil obedience? Certainly, if obedience to the state involves disobedience to God, Christians must obey God rather than man (Acts 5:29).

Acts of Civil Disobedience

Scripture provides us with a number of precedents for refusing to obey the state. For example, when Pharaoh told the Hebrew midwives to kill the newborn boys, they refused to obey:

> The midwives ... feared God and did not do what the king of Egypt had told them to do; they let the boys live.
>
> (Exodus 1:17)

Rahab risked her life by turning against her own people and hiding the Israelite spies (Joshua 2:6); Obadiah secretly protected the Lord's prophets, contrary to the orders of Queen Jezebel (1 Kings 18:3–13); Jeremiah publicly defied the policy of King Zedekiah by telling the people of Jerusalem to surrender to the Babylonians, rather than fight, and as a result was considered to be a traitor (Jeremiah 38:1–4); Daniel and his three friends refused, in defiance of state policy, to accept the royal food and wine because it was ceremonially unclean (Daniel 1); Shadrach, Meshach and Abednego refused to worship the image of gold that King Nebuchadnezzar had set up, preferring to be incinerated in the fiery furnace rather than disobey God (Daniel 3); Daniel refused to address prayer to King Darius as a god, even though this was state policy for only thirty days, and continued to pray three times a day, just as he had always done, giving thanks to his God, despite the consequences of the lions' den (Daniel 6).

The New Testament reveals that when the Sanhedrin commanded the apostles not to speak or teach in the name of Jesus, they refused to comply (Acts 4:18–20; 5:29). Indeed, it is from Acts 4:19 that those who engage in civil disobedience for religious reasons find their standard text:

> "Judge for yourselves whether it is right in God's sight to obey you rather than God."

To give just one example from modern history, during the Second World War, Corrie ten Boom, in Nazi-occupied Holland, disobeyed the government by hiding Jews and protecting them in defiance of the state. She was one of many who risked everything to protect innocent victims from a ruthless regime. In each of these instances civil disobedience was clearly justified. Even so, there is always a temptation to base decisions upon a desire for comfort rather than conviction. Adolph Hitler's totalitarianism was undoubtedly aided and abetted partly by Christians who accepted what he said.

Final Considerations

Having considered the overall situation, albeit briefly, it is now possible to evaluate the finer detail and by using God's infallible and sufficient Word aim to provide a consistent picture. No attempt is made to examine every example of biblical warfare. There are so many that it would undoubtedly and unnecessarily create confusion. Rather, the aim is to consider the prominent underlying principles of why God reacted in the way that He did in specific situations. The next chapter examines how God sometimes told His people to go to war and fought for them.

Summary

Studying the Old and New Testaments could easily leave you with the impression that they speak a totally different message. This would be a grave mistake. The recurring theme in Matthew 5, "You have heard that it was said ... But I tell you," does not contradict or invalidate the Old Testament Law or the Prophets (Matthew 5:17). Rather it corrects misinterpretations and the legalistic emphasis on externals that were prominent in Jesus' time.

God's character does not change; He is the same Lord, yesterday, today and forever (Hebrews 13:8). God never abandons justice in favor of mercy. Otherwise the supreme sacrifice of His Son on our behalf would have been unnecessary. Jesus who allowed Himself to be led like a lamb to the slaughter for our sins will one day return to judge justly and wage war against His enemies. Love and the pursuit of justice are not inseparable.

Christians must live as followers of Jesus. Therefore, acts of civil disobedience may on occasion be permissible and even mandatory so as to achieve a change in government policy. This should always be done in a conscientious and non-violent manner, so distinguishing it from an act of insurrection or revolution.

To think about and discuss

1. Why is it vital to have an overall picture prior to examining the minute detail?

2. Although the greatest of Israel's kings, David, was guilty of heinous crimes (2 Samuel 11), he was described as a man after God's own heart (1 Samuel 13:14 and quoted in Acts 13:22). What do we learn from this?

3. Jesus chose to enter Jerusalem on a donkey. Next time He will be riding a white horse. Why on that occasion will it be inappropriate for Him to ride on a donkey?

4. Under what circumstances can a Christian justify civil disobedience? Can you think of circumstances from your own experience?

God Fights for His People

Because God had chosen the Israelites to be His treasured possession (Deuteronomy 14:2), and had made a covenant with them (Exodus 19:5–6), it was vital that He gave them victory over their many enemies. Otherwise this small nation would have been quickly annihilated by its more powerful neighbors. Hence, there are numerous instances within the Bible where God fought for His people, thus guaranteeing their survival. The dual aim of this chapter is to examine some of these examples, and then to try and understand why God acted in the way that He did.

Escape through the Red Sea

Undoubtedly one of the most familiar accounts of God fighting for His people was when they escaped through the Red Sea on dry ground (Exodus 14). Moses told the people,

> "The LORD will fight for you; you need only to be still."
>
> (v. 14)

They did not have to defend themselves or fight. Even so, it appeared to the average Israelite to be a desperate, if not hopeless situation. Before them was the Red Sea, whilst to their rear they could see the Egyptian army marching after them. Consequently, they cried out to the Lord, not in faith but in fear. This was the time for God to act:

> Then the angel of God, who had been traveling in front of Israel's army, withdrew and went behind them ... coming between the armies of Egypt and Israel. Throughout the night the cloud brought darkness to one side and light to the other; so neither went near the other all night long. Then Moses stretched out his hand over the sea, and all that night the LORD drove the sea back with a strong east wind and turned it into dry land. The waters were divided and the Israelites went through the sea on dry ground, with a wall of water on their right and on their left.
>
> (vv. 19–22)

The exact nature of this event has been the subject of much imaginative and futile speculation which need not concern us, for it is better to concentrate only upon the facts. In this instance, natural means provided an unnatural effect because of a supernatural cause. That is, a strong east wind created a passage through the sea at exactly the right time manifestly displaying God's almighty power. It was one of the most remarkable and vital miracles in the Old Testament, for it enabled the Israelites to pass through the sea on dry ground whilst hotly pursued by the Egyptians who soon encountered serious problems. Psalm 77:17 indicates that a cloudburst, which again was a sign of God's power, helped to hinder the chariots' movements. Confusion prevailed and the Egyptians tried to escape, but it was too late. Moses was told by the Lord to stretch out his hand over the sea so that the army of Pharaoh would be drowned, and that is what happened. The Israelites looking back saw the dead bodies of the Egyptians washed up on the shore. Not one of them survived.

Some might consider the drowning of the Egyptians to be a just punishment for them having drowned the baby boys of the Israelites in the Nile (Exodus 1:22). Doesn't the Bible often teach the strict law of equal retribution? You are to take eye for eye and life for life. Others will find it repugnant and extremely difficult to comprehend how a God of love can enforce such a severe and apparently indiscriminate punishment. Before considering these contrasting views there are other examples of God fighting for His people that need to be examined.

Israel Defeats the Amalekites

After crossing the Red Sea the Israelites were attacked for the first time on their wilderness journey by the vicious Amalekites at Rephidim (Exodus 17:8–13). In the battle everything progressed well for Israel as long as Moses held up the staff of God, but if he lowered it the Amalekites were stronger. Therefore, Israel's strength was obviously dependent upon a continuous appeal to God without whose power they could achieve nothing. However, it should be noted that this did not exclude Joshua's action. He and his men had to fight with the sword even though God had assured them of victory. This was acknowledged by Moses in the name he gave to the altar he built, "Jehovah-Nissi," which literally means "The Lord is my banner," a reference to the fact that God had given them victory over their enemies.

Joshua

Another miracle relating to water is when the Israelites crossed the River Jordan prior to attacking Jericho (Joshua 3). This

Canaanite stronghold appeared to be impregnable, and its inhabitants confidently relied on the strong city walls for protection. The Israelite soldiers had no experience of attacking such a fortress, but the Lord had told Joshua,

> "See, I have delivered Jericho into your hands, along with its king and its fighting men."
>
> (Joshua 6:2)

The Israelites were to obey, and God by His miraculous power would provide the means. All the Israelite soldiers needed to do was to march around the city once on six successive days, and then seven times on the seventh day. After their final circuit the priests who accompanied the army and marched ahead of the ark would sound a long blast on the trumpets. This signaled that the people were to give a loud shout, and the walls of Jericho would collapse allowing the Israelites to enter the city freely from all sides.

They shouted as loudly as they could and suddenly the walls of Jericho collapsed. Since no serious resistance was encountered, the Israelites easily completed their task:

> They devoted the city to the LORD and destroyed with the sword every living thing in it – men and women, young and old, cattle, sheep and donkeys.
>
> (Joshua 6:21)

Only Rahab the prostitute and those with her were spared because of an earlier promise given by two spies (Joshua 2:12–14). The whole city and everything in it was burned except for the things which were placed in the treasury of the Lord's house. Jericho was given to Israel by the Lord so that they might devote it back to Him.

Following the death of Joshua and during the period when Israel was ruled by judges, there were conflicts within the nation and wars with their neighbors. Repeatedly one observes God fighting for His people using leaders such as Barak, Gideon, Jephthah and Samson. All these are mentioned by the author of the Letter to the Hebrews as men of faith and are therefore worthy of careful study.

Saul's Sin and Rejection

The Amalekites, who were descendants of Esau's grandson Amalek (Genesis 36:12), were in conflict with Israel on several occasions. Remember that they had been the first people to attack the Israelites on their way to Canaan at Rephidim. God had declared that He would "blot out the memory of Amalek from under heaven" (Exodus 17:14). This evil nation needed to be dealt with once and for all and for this reason God commands Saul, through Samuel, to exterminate them.

> "This is what the LORD Almighty says: 'I will punish the Amalekites for what they did to Israel when they waylaid them as they came up from Egypt. Now go, attack the Amalekites and totally destroy everything that belongs to them. Do not spare them; put to death men and women, children and infants, cattle and sheep, camels and donkeys.'"
>
> (1 Samuel 15:2–3)

Consequently, Saul summoned his forces and attacked the Amalekites, destroying them with the sword, except for Agag their king and "the best of the sheep and cattle, the fat calves and lambs – everything that was good." It is also apparent that some of the Amalekites must have escaped since they were not wiped out until the reign of Hezekiah (1 Chronicles 4:43).

Saul had blatantly disobeyed the Lord and though he seemed oblivious to this (1 Samuel 15:13), the sheep were bleating a different story! He had rejected the word of the Lord and so the Lord would reject him as king over Israel. David son of Jesse was anointed king, though it would be many years before he ascended the throne.

David, a Man of God

The final example to be considered before examining why God acted in the way that He did, is the time when David fought Goliath. The Philistine army had moved eastwards from their stronghold of Gath and crossed the Israelite frontier near Socoh in the Valley of Elah. Here they were confronted by the army of Israel. A situation arose in which the two opponents found themselves lined up on opposite sides of the valley with neither side wanting to make the first move. One way in which the armies of the day resolved such situations of deadlock was for each side to send out a champion to fight on their behalf, and the winner would then claim whatever at that time was being disputed. In this instance at stake was the sovereignty of Israel.

The Philistine champion, Goliath, was a man of giant stature of whom the Israelites were terrified. Although they did not surrender or withdraw they had no idea what to do next. Each day for forty days, morning and evening Goliath challenged Israel and there was no response. Then into this situation stepped young David who was confident of victory. If there was ever a physical mismatch, this was it. However, what might seem to be impossible for man is possible with God. Paul writing to the Philippians says:

"I can do everything through him who gives me strength."

(4:13)

David took his staff, his sling and five smooth stones and approached Goliath. Meanwhile, Goliath, with his shield bearer in front of him, kept coming closer, and when he saw that his opposition was only a boy he despised him. David was not frightened because faith always conquers fear and so he could say:

> "You come against me with sword and spear and javelin, but I come against you in the name of the LORD Almighty, the God of the armies of Israel, whom you have defied. This day the LORD will hand you over to me, and I'll strike you down and cut off your head. Today I will give the carcasses of the Philistine army to the birds of the air and the beasts of the earth, and the whole world will know that there is a God in Israel. All those gathered here will know that it is not by sword or spear that the LORD saves; for the battle is the LORD's, and he will give all of you into our hands."
>
> (1 Samuel 17:45–47)

As far as David was concerned the outcome was a forgone conclusion, not because of his own greatness but because of God's power. With one stone from David's sling Goliath was felled and then decapitated with his own sword. Goliath had been blasphemous, arrogant and over-confident, and he had underestimated the enemy, which is always a fatal error in warfare. How often the mighty have fallen.

When the Philistines saw that their hero was dead they turned and ran, hotly pursued by the men of Israel and Judah who were now no longer afraid. They had seen how God could use an ordinary man to achieve what appeared to be an impossible task. One smooth stone in the hand of a man of God resulted in victory, and David became the nation's hero. When the victorious Israelite army returned home the women

came out singing and dancing for joy. Their song included the
lines:

> "Saul has slain his thousands,
>   and David his tens of thousands."

(1 Samuel 18:7)

David would become a great soldier and successfully fight
many battles in the name of God.

Difficult Questions

Having considered various examples of God fighting for His
people, several difficult questions arise. Perhaps the most
pressing for many will be: how does one react to a God who
appears to be harsh and indiscriminate? The Egyptians were
drowned in the Red Sea en masse. Water that is so essential for
sustaining human life is so often the cause of death and
destruction. The tsunami of December 2004 was a vivid
reminder of this and should make us as human beings realize
our dependence upon God. We also need to be mindful of the
truth that He destroys that which is wicked.

Having said that, it is important to appreciate that God's
judgment does not mean that all who suffer are guilty of the
same degree of idolatry and corruption. Jesus makes it abundantly clear that personal disaster is not necessarily the result of
some secret heinous sin (Luke 13:1–5). Books such as Job and
Ecclesiastes also reveal that punishment can be disproportion-
ate to the crime. In this life the wicked often prosper whilst the
righteous suffer. Stephen was stoned to death, John the Baptist
was beheaded, James died by the sword; numerous Christians
have been burnt at the stake or thrown to the lions because of
their faith.

Certain parts of the Bible undoubtedly create major problems for many. Why was it necessary for God to exterminate a whole people such as the Amalekites and even their animals (1 Samuel 15:3)? The inclusion of women and children appears barbaric and the addition of livestock bizarre. It will not win favor with the animal rights activists. Such action can appear to be unnecessary and exceptionally harsh. A person will sometimes say, "I cannot believe in a God who lets such things happen." However, a failure to accept this reveals an unawareness of our awesome and sovereign God.

The Ban

The violence associated with the worship of God by the Israelites is conspicuously illustrated by the ban (Hebrew: *herem*), the practice whereby the defeated enemy was sacrificed to God. In 1 Samuel 15:3 the New International Version uses the words "totally destroy" to convey the sense of *herem*, which signified a complete dedication to God of any who had offended against Him. The Amalekites had been placed under a *herem* because they had attacked the Israelites during their wilderness wanderings (Exodus 17:8ff.). God wanted them destroyed because they indulged in all kinds of detestable practices which He hates and which constituted an habitual threat to the purity of His people. Hence, their extermination was inevitable. It was because Saul disobeyed God by failing to exterminate them that the Israelites did not fully possess the Promised Land for several centuries. A major factor in their eventual downfall was, of course, their participation in the idolatry of the nations they should have destroyed, a danger of which they had been forewarned (Deuteronomy 20:16–18).

In the Bible, as we have just seen, one observes that in the majority of cases the *herem* was carried out at God's command.

There were other instances when the *herem* was undertaken on human initiative. In Numbers 21:1–3, for example, the Israelites, having encountered a setback at Arad, make the following vow to the Lord:

> "If you will deliver these people into our hands, we will totally destroy their cities." The LORD listened to Israel's plea and gave the Canaanites over to them. They completely destroyed them and their towns; so the place was named Hormah.
>
> (vv. 2–3)

Hormah means "destruction." Obviously more than the destruction of property was involved.

Although many people today find the concept of the *herem* difficult to understand or accept, it would not have posed a problem to the Israelites or some of their neighbors. As one example, similar terminology is used by the Moabite king Mesha of the mid ninth-century BC. A Moabite Stone exhibited in the Louvre, Paris, describes how cultic equipment used in worship of the God of Israel, which has been seized in war, is presented to the god Chemosh and all Israelite inhabitants of Ataroth and Nebo are "devoted" – slain for divine satisfaction.

Few people have ever taken the *herem* texts of the Hebrew Bible as commandments for their own time. Rather they are interpreted as applying to specific races that no longer exist. It would be a grave mistake to believe that chapters such as 1 Samuel 15 are a justification today for ethnic cleansing. Then it was an essential act in the history of redemption, but since Jesus came into the world the situation has changed. New Testament passages like John 3 and Hebrews 10 clearly reveal that holiness is attained through His death and resurrection, not through the eradication of those who offend God. God does not take pleasure from the death of human beings, even if they are wicked, and neither should we. Like Him we should long for them to return from their wicked ways so that they might live (Ezekiel 33:11). Our aim should be to live in peace with everyone, as far as it is possible.

Summary

"The LORD is a warrior," says the Song of Moses (Exodus 15:3). He had proved it by hurling Pharaoh's chariots and army into the sea. God's people were involved in numerous wars, sometimes at His explicit command and sometimes winning victory by supernatural means. However, the Bible never portrays God as gaining pleasure from the death of the wicked. Quite the contrary, the continuing theme is of God's extreme patience and abounding love, of His hatred of human wars. His judgment was always an act of last resort undertaken when the moral depravity of a nation became so great that it was irreversible. Only then did God decide to destroy it. He had no alternative, since allowing the wickedness to continue would have meant that He had to deny His own just character and righteousness. A holy God must eventually punish all sin.

To think about and discuss

1. The Lord's command was clear: the Amalekites were to be destroyed, "men and women, children and infants, cattle and sheep, camels and donkeys" (1 Samuel 15:3). Why was this necessary?
2. Is the above situation applicable today? If not, why not?
3. The belief that personal disaster is the result of personal sin was entrenched in the consciousness of the Jew; see, for example, Job 4:7 and John 9:2. Discuss why Jesus

refutes this (Luke 13:1–2) and why any who do not repent will perish.

4. "No king is saved by the size of his army, no warrior escapes by his great strength" (Psalm 33:16). When David defeated Goliath it was God's victory. Why should Christians not depend upon military power for their security?

God Fights Against His People

An examination of the Bible reveals that God not only fought for His people, but on several occasions declared war against them because of their many transgressions. Accordingly, in Amos 2:4–3:15 the prophet lists the rebellions of Judah and Israel alongside those of six heathen nations, and all would be severely punished. While the heathen nations would be punished for their excessive cruelty, Judah and Israel were guilty of repeatedly sinning against God, despite all He had done for them. The Israelites were often punished because they did evil in the eyes of the Lord and did not serve Him as they ought.

It should be remembered that the Israelites owed their existence as a nation to the Lord alone. They were His people for He had made a covenant with them which He would never break; but He had attached conditions to it. He had clearly commanded that the Canaanites and anything connected with their religion must be totally destroyed (Deuteronomy 7:2–6; Joshua 23:12–13). This was a necessary punishment for their sins and essential to prevent them being a spiritual threat to Israel. All the Israelites had to do was to obey God and a glorious future awaited them.

This was not to be for history clearly shows that the terms of God's covenant were ignored. The Canaanites were not destroyed and so their idolatrous practice of Baal worship spread. The Israelites erroneously and foolishly fell into the belief that adherence to Baal, the god who supposedly controlled rain and storm, would result in economic prosperity (Hosea 2:5, 8). Their desire to worship created things rather than the Creator was a terrible mistake. It was because of their infidelity, and a refusal to acknowledge the true source of the blessings bestowed upon them, that they forfeited their rights. Consequently, God said, "I will do to you what I plan to do to them" (Numbers 33:56), that is, dispossess them.

God was angry with His people. He had promised to go before them and fight their battles. Already God had brought His people out of bondage in Egypt, but they were not grateful. During the wilderness journey they were often dissatisfied and grumbled. Whenever a problem arose they wallowed in self-pity and failed to look to God. Even when standing on the threshold of Canaan the people rebelled against God's guidance.

Moses prudently sent out twelve spies – one from each tribe – to explore and establish the best route to take. This reconnaissance took forty days. When the spies returned they accurately reported their findings to Moses, Aaron and the people of Israel (Numbers 13:26–33). It was, indeed, a magnificent and fertile country as the Lord had promised. However, the people living there were powerful; the cities were fortified and very large. How would they respond to such a challenge? It was God's promises versus their opponents' power.

One of the spies, called Caleb, tried to encourage the people as they stood before Moses. He was confident that they could conquer the land. Nevertheless, others who had explored the land with him objected: "We seemed like grasshoppers in our own eyes, and we looked the same to them" (v. 33). They considered the opposition to be too strong. Their defeatist attitude discouraged the Israelites. Instead of listening to God they listened to the jaundiced opinions of men. The size of the problem appeared to be too great because they lacked faith in God and so succumbed to unbelief. God had previously protected and provided for them and yet they treated Him with contempt. He had promised them victory and therefore it was right to fight, but they stubbornly disobeyed. It was a lost opportunity.

Sometimes their slavery in Egypt appeared preferable to their present situation. Why was the Lord taking them to this country only for them to die in battle? Why not return to Egypt? Since Moses would certainly have been against such a course of action, the answer was to choose another leader (Numbers 14:4). How would God react in this situation? He would disown and destroy them. What about the promise to Abram and his descendants? This still applied for a new people would replace them. The next generation would not be deprived of their birthright because of their parents' sins. Although the Lord repeatedly chastised His people they were never abandoned.

Moses appealed to God's mercy and the people were once again forgiven, but any who were twenty years old or older and had been counted in the census would not enter the land promised to their ancestors. Only Caleb and Joshua of the twelve spies would live to inherit it. The Israelites had said that it would be better to die in the wilderness than from the opposition that would be encountered on entering Canaan. Hence, their wish would be granted. They would be forced to wander in the desert because of their disobedience, whilst the ten spies who had incited the rebellion were struck dead with a plague.

Again the Israelites behaved foolishly. Rather than repent and desire to do God's will, they went from one foolish extreme to the other. Now they would attempt the conquest of Canaan despite God having clearly said that none of the fighting men except Caleb and Joshua would ever enter the land. It was forbidden territory. Moses, who knew the Lord better than they, warned them not to go, but without success. He knew that because the Lord was not with them, defeat was inevitable (Numbers 14:43). Not only were they now fighting against the Amalekites and Canaanites, but against the Lord's will. Therefore, neither Moses nor the ark of the Lord's covenant would accompany them on this occasion, as was normal when Israel went into battle. Hence, it should be no surprise that they paid a great price, for the result was an overwhelming defeat which drove them back into the wilderness.

The Book of Deuteronomy concludes with the death of Moses. Because of his sin (Numbers 20:12) Moses was not permitted to cross with the people into the Promised Land, but he was allowed to see it. He went to Mount Nebo on the plains of Moab and climbed Pisgah Peak which is across from Jericho. From there the Lord showed him the Promised Land. Moses died in the land of Moab and was buried in a valley near Beth-peor.

Joshua and the Promised Land

Joshua, the son of Nun, who had played a prominent part on several occasions during the wilderness journey, now succeeds Moses. He was God's choice for the task ahead of leading the Israelites to victory. Behind them now was the harsh experience of the desert, whilst before them lay the glorious prospect of Canaan.

Although the Book of Joshua is mainly the account of

Israelite conquest because they served the Lord faithfully, it also reveals a few problems. For example, following their defeat of formidable Jericho is the story of Achan and a humiliating defeat at Ai (Joshua 7:1–26). The Israelites acted unfaithfully in regard to the devoted things and so the Lord's anger burned against them. Achan's violation of the ban defiled all Israel and brought judgment upon them for not having given the Lord what belonged to Him.

Joshua and the elders of Israel realized that there must be a hidden reason for this ignominious defeat. They knew that the honor of God's name required that His people be victorious. Why should the Lord have brought Israel this far only to allow them to be destroyed by the Amorites? Something had gone seriously wrong and there was only one reasonable answer to rectify the problem. Joshua prayed and the Lord answered.

Achan was revealed to be guilty of violating the covenant of the Lord. Immediately Joshua and Israel executed the ban as God had commanded (v. 15). Achan and all his family were stoned to death and their possessions destroyed. Then the bodies were burnt and covered with a large heap of stones which would serve as a warning to succeeding generations. The Lord's anger which had burned fiercely was now appeased.

The Israelites' defeat at Ai reveals that God would not always grant victory and prosperity to His chosen people. God's primary concern was the honor of His name and if the Israelites sinned, they like anyone else would be punished. The overall message of Joshua, however, is not one primarily of warning but one of enjoyment and encouragement. Israel is shown to be the army of the living God, led by the Lord Himself to many victories. The possession of the Promised Land is assured and they could have expected continuing blessing had they obeyed God. Sadly they did not.

Days of the Judges

The Book of Judges portrays a picture of Israel that differs considerably from that of the Book of Joshua, because of sin. "The Israelites did evil in the eyes of the LORD" is repeated seven times (Judges 2:11; 3:7; 3:12; 4:1; 6:1; 10:6 and 13:1). It is no wonder that God became angry. They repeatedly refused to obey and were punished:

> In his anger against Israel the LORD handed them over to raiders who plundered them. He sold them to their enemies all around, whom they were no longer able to resist. Whenever Israel went out to fight, the hand of the LORD was against them to defeat them. They were in great distress.
>
> (Judges 2:14–15)

This situation was entirely the Israelites' own fault for God had repeatedly warned them of the severe consequences of worshiping false gods. Occasionally this led to a time of brief repentance but it never significantly changed the course on which they had embarked. There were successive periods of rebellion, retribution, repentance and then, by God's grace, restoration. After sinning and being punished by a foreign oppressor, Israel was delivered by a judge raised up by God.

The Northern Tribes' Revolt

Undoubtedly 1 Kings 12 records one of the major events of the Old Testament, namely the division of the nation of Israel into two parts. Grave mistakes were made both by Rehoboam, in his attitude towards the request of the northern tribes, and by Israel, in their response of abandoning the House of David.

Neither is surprising considering that there was no attempt to seek the will of God as had been done on many previous occasions to decide vital issues (e.g. Joshua 24:1; 1 Samuel 10:19; 2 Chronicles 29:20–21).

A kingdom that is divided is very vulnerable to attack and they did not have to wait long. In the fifth year of Rehoboam's reign, the king of Egypt (Sheshonq 1, *c.* 945–24 BC) attacked Jerusalem. The temple and the royal palace were stripped of their treasures, including the shields of gold which Solomon had made (1 Kings 14:25–26). This was rightly considered to be a sign of divine punishment and resulted in a temporary reformation (2 Chronicles 12:2–12). After attacking Judah, Shishak, who previously had given asylum to Jeroboam when he fled from Solomon, marched through Jeroboam's territory and caused mass destruction of life and property.

Jeroboam and his successors were all wicked men and for this reason blessing was withheld. It was inevitable that their persistent spiritual blindness would one day be severely punished for God had often warned them of the consequences of their sin. The house of Omri was warned by the prophets Elijah and Elisha, and the house of Jehu, during the prosperous time of Jeroboam II, by Amos and Hosea.

Despite their repeated warnings about the obvious dangers of indifference and spiritual complacency the people refused to listen. Hence, in 724 BC the Assyrian monarch Shalmaneser V attacked Israel and Hoshea, their last king, was captured and imprisoned (2 Kings 17:1–6). Samaria, the capital, was placed under siege, and since the king was already caught, they no doubt expected that it would soon be taken. However, it was not until 722 BC that Samaria fell and Israel ceased to exist as a sovereign power.

The Kingdom of Judah

Judah's history ran parallel to that of Israel but was extended by almost a century and a half. During that time there were some good kings such as Hezekiah and Josiah who found favor with God. Unfortunately their immense, constructive religious reforms were only transient and the Judeans constantly lapsed back into disobedience. The prophet Isaiah and then Jeremiah had repeatedly denounced sin and warned of the judgment to come:

> But they mocked God's messengers, despised his words and scoffed at his prophets until the wrath of the LORD was aroused against his people and there was no remedy.
>
> (2 Chronicles 36:16)

The dominance of the Assyrian empire was a major threat to Judah and her neighbors. Consequently, Hezekiah and other allied kings challenged Assyria during the reign of Sennacherib (705–681 BC) with disastrous results. Many Judean cities and villages were destroyed, though Jerusalem miraculously survived (2 Kings 19:35–36).

During the latter years of its empire Assyria formed an alliance with Egypt, but it was not enough to maintain its position of supremacy. Early in 605 BC at the Battle of Carchemish on the Euphrates, Nebuchadnezzar was victorious and Babylonia (in modern-day Iraq) became the new world power. Nebuchadnezzar moved as far south as Jerusalem and forced Jehoiakim and other kings of the area into submission. Among men taken captive from Jerusalem to distant Babylon were Daniel and his friends Hananiah, Mishael and Azariah.

There was a brief interlude during which Nebuchadnezzar withdrew because of the death of his father Nabopolassar in

August 605 BC, but he returned with a vengeance. This was because Jehoiakim had rebelled and looked to Egypt for support (2 Kings 24:1). He died whilst Jerusalem was under Babylonian siege and so his son Jehoiachin was on the throne when the city fell in March 597 BC. Jehoiachin and many others were exiled to Babylon, including the prophet Ezekiel.

Nebuchadnezzar placed Mattaniah, whose name he changed to Zedekiah, on the throne, but he proved to be disloyal. As a result Nebuchadnezzar and his army again attacked Jerusalem and it fell in July 586 BC. The city was plundered and its treasures taken to Babylon. It is clear from 2 Chronicles 36:17 that this was the judgment of God.

The Babylonians set fire to God's temple, built by Solomon four centuries earlier, broke down the wall of Jerusalem and burned all the palaces. Those people of any significance who escaped from the sword were taken into exile and became servants until the kingdom of Persia came to power. This once beautiful city was now desolate. The temple symbolic of God's presence and glory was now destroyed. Only the poorest of Jerusalem's people were left behind, ensuring that it would probably be impossible to organize a successful revolt against Babylon in the future. As an independent kingdom Judah was finished, though its history would continue.

The Book of Lamentations, a sequel to Jeremiah's prophecy, mourns the destruction of Jerusalem in 586 BC and the deplorable condition of Israel. Daniel the prophet, who held high government posts, and Ezekiel, known as "The Prophet of Visions," both ministered during this time of captivity.

When God called Ezekiel to be a prophet, He warned him of the difficult task ahead because the Israelites remained "a rebellious nation that has rebelled against me; they and their fathers have been in revolt against me to this very day. The people to whom I am sending you are obstinate and stubborn"

(Ezekiel 2:3–4). Even so, there is always hope when God's word is preached. The very fact that Ezekiel was in Babylon ministering to Judah was an indication that God had not abandoned His people.

Subsequent history shows this to be true. God does not forsake His people. But neither does He tolerate sinful acts. The Israelites were severely punished so that they might realize the seriousness of their sin and repent. It's a simple choice: either love the Lord your God and be blessed, or worship false gods and be punished. This is a recurring and ongoing cycle because the God of the Old Testament and the God of the New Testament are one and the same. Judgment will certainly come upon all who reject Christ, for a holy God cannot live with unholy people. War in the Old Testament was always related to judgment and wickedness.

Summary

God delivered the Israelites from the Egyptians and established them in a spacious land flowing with milk and honey (Exodus 3:8). A glorious future lay ahead of them. Were they thankful for this? No, they were not. Repeatedly they did evil in the eyes of the Lord. Israel was a land of idolatry and rebellion, of oppression and exploitation. The prophets, who understood the implications of the people's behavior, proclaimed that God's promise of protection, given in the covenant, was conditional upon their obedience. Unfortunately, they did not listen and so their spiritual complacency was punished. Clearly God does not have one set of rules for His chosen people and another set for everyone else. Israel was left in no doubt that God honors His threats as well as His promises; He strictly adheres to what He says. He will punish everyone who does not turn from their own way and embrace the ways of God.

There is no alternative to this truth, for to dilute God's wrath is to diminish God's holiness. Despite the Israelites being severely punished by God, it is evident that His ultimate aim was to lead His people to repentance. The important lesson we need to learn is how to avoid the failures of God's people in the past and instead repeat their victories.

To think about and discuss

1. How does faith in God affect the way I live? How can my faith be strengthened?
2. What are the rewards of faithfulness? Why should I be faithful?
3. Why does God punish His people?
4. Will God ever abandon His people? How can I be assured of God's care for me in difficult times?

CHAPTER

Spiritual Warfare

6

Within the Old Testament war usually refers to a physical struggle between nations, whereas in the New Testament it more often applies to spiritual conflict between good and evil. It is very obvious that the major problem for the Christian is warfare not against enemies of flesh and blood, but rather against formidable evil spiritual forces intent on destroying God's redemptive work (Ephesians 6:12). Hence, there is a great danger in being a Christian within an unchristian society.

Persecution should be expected by everyone who earnestly desires to live a godly life in Christ Jesus (2 Timothy 3:12). Christ said:

> "If the world hates you, keep in mind that it hated me first. If you belonged to the world, it would love you as its own. As it is, you do not belong to the world, but I have chosen you out of the world. That is why the world hates you. Remember the words I spoke to you: 'No servant is greater than his master.' If they persecuted me, they will persecute you also."
>
> (John 15:18–20; cf. 16:33)

Despite this certain persecution, God has not abandoned His people, for He gives power to those who seek Him (Acts 4:31) and obey Him (Acts 5:32).

The coming of the Holy Spirit at Pentecost (Acts 2:1–21) was the dawn of a new era and fulfilled the promise of Jesus to the apostles that they would be baptized with the Holy Spirit (John 16:7; Acts 1:5). On the Day of Pentecost the believers were meeting together in one place. Suddenly, there was a sound from heaven like the blowing of a violent wind, and it filled the house where they were meeting. This mighty sound was undoubtedly indicative of a vast supernatural power. When God's Spirit blows, a dead situation becomes alive and extraordinary things happen. It has always been so.

The prophet Ezekiel, as the result of the activity of the Holy Spirit, had a vision of a valley full of very dry bones (Ezekiel 37:1–14). Then God asked him a crucial question: "Can these bones live?" (v. 3). Ezekiel answered very carefully, "O Sovereign LORD, you alone know." If anyone other than God had asked the question, Ezekiel would have immediately responded by saying that the situation was hopeless. Dry bones do not naturally come to life, but he understood enough about God to know that nothing was actually impossible. The Lord told him to prophesy to the breath, saying, "Come from the four winds, O breath, and breathe into these slain, that they may live" (v. 9). When he did this, the breath entered into their bodies and they stood up on their feet – a vast army. In this vision Ezekiel saw a desolate picture of his own people (v. 11), and what God could do with a desperate situation. The Spirit of God breathed into them new life.

In John 3 the story is told of a highly regarded religious teacher called Nicodemus who came to Jesus to ask Him questions. He didn't understand how the Holy Spirit gives new life from heaven. Jesus answered him:

"The wind blows wherever it pleases. You hear its sound, but
you cannot tell where it comes from or where it is going. So it
is with everyone born of the Spirit."

(v. 8)

However, nobody can have the Spirit poured out on them and
not be aware of the experience. Then, and now, people are
miraculously changed as the Spirit enters their lives.

On the Day of Pentecost there also appeared what seemed to
be tongues of fire descending from above; they separated and
came to rest on each of the believers praying together. Fire is
frequently a symbol of God's presence. Moses saw a bush ablaze
with fire and was amazed because it didn't burn up (Exodus 3).
He realized that it was supernatural fire and once his attention
was caught, God called to him from the bush. God guided His
people at night by a pillar of fire (Exodus 13). It was the fire of
the Lord that fell and burned up the sacrifice of Elijah at Mount
Carmel (1 Kings 18:38). Fire consumed Ahaziah's captains and
their men (2 Kings 1:10, 12) and later it was a chariot of fire
that appeared just before Elijah was taken up to heaven in a
whirlwind (2 Kings 2:11). "Our God is a consuming fire" were
words spoken by Moses when he exhorted the Israelites against
idolatry (Deuteronomy 4:24; cf. 9:3; Hebrews 12:29).

The worship of false gods is applicable today, for idols which
are substitutes for God need not necessarily be made of wood,
stone or metal. Examples of present-day idolatries include the
adoration of pleasure, of prosperity, and of power and prestige.
Anything that comes between self and a holy God is idolatrous
and will eventually be punished by the fire of His righteous
judgment. Repeatedly in the Bible, fire is a symbol of purity and
purification.

John the Baptist had said, "I baptize you with water for
repentance ... He [Jesus] will baptize you with the Holy Spirit

and with fire" (Matthew 3:11). That is exactly what happened at Pentecost. The believers were touched by what appeared to be tongues of fire and began to speak coherent words in languages they had never learnt. Humanly speaking this would be impossible, but supernaturally it was no problem. God was bypassing their intellect and giving their mouths words to declare the wonderful things He has done.

These believers experienced three things which appear natural: wind, fire and speech, but were supernatural both in origin and character. What they heard wasn't wind, but sounded like it; what they saw wasn't fire, but resembled it; and what they spoke was in languages unfamiliar to them. They heard, saw and spoke, but what they *experienced* was more than sensory. The power of the Holy Spirit had come and so it was impossible for them not to glorify Jesus.

Despite the overwhelming evidence, there were those who refused to accept the truth. Seeing does not necessarily lead to believing. Therefore, it should be no surprise to discover that some made fun of the believers and accused them of being drunk (Acts 2:13). They were attempting to find an improbable natural answer for a supernatural occurrence.

It is true that there are similarities between being intoxicated by alcohol and being filled with the Holy Spirit. In both instances one overcomes self-consciousness and so is better able to establish relationships with others. However, there is a vital difference between the two. Intoxication through alcohol results in a loss of control of normal mental and physical functions. This is contrary to self-control which is a characteristic of the Holy Spirit (Galatians 5:23). To avoid any possible confusion Peter explains that they are not drunk but that it is something promised by God centuries before through the prophet Joel. In the last days, God says, "I will pour out my Spirit on all people" (Joel 2:28).

There is a final period in our history called "the last days." They began when the Spirit came at Pentecost and will end on the great and glorious day when the Lord returns. The period between the two comings, the period in which we live, is the age when the Spirit will be poured out on all people. This applies to everyone irrespective of their age, sex or social status. The only requirement is that it must be received by repentance and faith.

Between the Day of Pentecost and the Day of the Lord when Jesus will return is a period of great opportunity. A time during which the gospel of salvation will be preached throughout the world and all who call on the name of the Lord will be saved. God the Father planned it; Jesus Christ makes it possible; and it is the Holy Spirit that convicts people of their need of a Savior. It is only by the power of the Holy Spirit that anyone can come to faith in Christ.

Christians have a great commission to proclaim the gospel message. This task would be impossible if it were dependent on human resources alone. It can only be done by the power of the Holy Spirit. Zerubbabel who was in charge of rebuilding the temple became discouraged. How was he ever going to finish such an important task? It appeared to be physically impossible. Then the angel of the Lord spoke to him through the prophet Zechariah, " 'Not by might nor by power, but by my Spirit,' says the LORD Almighty" (Zechariah 4:6). God Himself will supply the necessary power.

The Christian life is a walk with God. It is to be actively involved in the front line of a battle and the only way to avoid defeat is to be strong in the Lord. In the Book of Judges we see that God imparted His Spirit upon such men as Othniel (3:10); Gideon (6:34); Jephthah (11:29); and Samson (13:25; 14:6, 19; 15:14, 19), thus enabling them to be victorious. Later in Israel's history, that was the reason for David's success. Samuel

anointed him to be king and from that day on the Spirit of the
Lord came upon him in power (1 Samuel 16:13), thus enabling
him to do many mighty things. In the New Testament Stephen
filled with the Holy Spirit had a vision of the glory of God (Acts
7:55). By the Spirit's power he was enabled to speak boldly
before the Jewish leaders and then courageously face martyrdom. Peter who had been just an ordinary fisherman could
speak effectively to a large crowd at Pentecost because of the
power of the Holy Spirit. Many of God's people have discovered that where the Holy Spirit intervenes there is no limit to
what can be achieved.

For instance, Gideon was called by the angel of the Lord
to deliver Israel from her enemies. With 32,000 men he
approached the Midianites (Judges 7). Before there was time
to attack, the Lord told Gideon that he had far too many
warriors with him. Therefore, any who were timid or afraid
were allowed to return home. More than two-thirds accepted
this opportunity, leaving only 10,000 who were willing to fight.
Again the Lord said that there were too many and that He
would choose who would go into battle. Only a tiny contingent
of 300 were retained, which makes it abundantly clear that
Israel was not to trust in her own strength or weapons. Victory
would be achieved not through military might but by the
power of God's Spirit. It also reveals that Gideon and those with
him were men of great faith.

Much can be accomplished by those who concentrate upon
the promises of God and step out in faith. In contrast those
who dwell on the present problems will experience periods of
difficulty; there will be a tremendous temptation to resign or
retreat from active service. A sad fact of life in many churches
today is that a faithful few appear to do all the work. Most
members, except for attending Sunday worship services when
convenient, are idle. Even though they may receive adequate

spiritual food, they are weak for lack of exercise and so neglect their God-given talents. They commit one of the greatest crimes of a soldier which is to fall asleep whilst on duty.

The Word of God clearly reveals that Christians are to be fighting in the name of God for the glory of God. They must stand firm against the devil's schemes despite the incessant hostilities. God never promises to take His soldiers out of the battle, not until they die. However, He does promise to provide all the resources which are essential to win so that they need never be discouraged or frightened. The sixteenth-century Scottish Reformer John Knox devised the phrase, "With God man is always in the majority." Paul said:

> "I can do everything through him who gives me strength."
>
> (Philippians 4:13)

If God be for us, it matters not who is against us. With the power of the Holy Spirit there is no problem which is too great.

Before going into battle the first necessity is to clearly identify the enemy. To be forewarned is to be forearmed. People who are antagonistic to Christianity are not the major threat for the main enemy is spiritual and therefore unseen (Ephesians 6:12). Peter portrays Satan as a prowling, roaring lion looking for someone to devour (1 Peter 5:8). The ruler of the kingdom of darkness even "masquerades as an angel of light" (2 Corinthians 11:14). As long as we are in the world we need to be constantly aware of Satan's subtle attacks. "Did God really say, 'You must not eat from any tree in the garden'?" (Genesis 3:1). His works are the same today as they were in the Garden of Eden. He questions the veracity of God's Word and then attempts to distort it.

Although a formidable opponent, Satan and the spiritual forces of evil are no match for God; but they are much stronger than God's people. Accordingly, this relentless battle requires that you find your inexhaustible strength in the Lord. Spiritual warfare must always be fought with spiritual weapons.

The Whole Armor of God

In 1655 the Puritan minister William Gurnall published his treatise *The Christian in Complete Armour*. The eighth edition of 1821 consists of three volumes, 261 chapters and 1,472 pages for an exposition of only eleven verses (Ephesians 6:10–20). Although extremely verbose, this classic is full of wise counsel. Dr Martyn Lloyd-Jones's two excellent volumes entitled *The Christian Warfare* and *The Christian Soldier* (Banner of Truth, 1977) cover the same eleven verses. These compilations of edited sermons preached in Westminster Chapel, London are an invaluable guide to living the Christian life.

For us as believers, the Holy Spirit is sent by the Father at the request of the Son (John 14:6) to supply whatever help is necessary. He fills us, taking control of our lives, providing that we remove any impediments and acknowledge our total dependence upon God. In spiritual warfare it is essential to put on the full armor of God (Ephesians 6:11–17). To leave any part exposed would be fatal for the enemy will always attack at the most vulnerable point. The belt of truth, the breastplate of righteousness, the gospel boots, the faith shield, salvation's helmet and the Spirit's sword are the six elements of the complete armor of God. These are readily available, but it is the Christian's responsibility to put them on. Only then can he or she go confidently into battle against the powers of evil.

Finally to the above list Paul adds prayer in the Spirit (Ephesians 6:18–20). It is necessary to pray at all times and on every occasion in the power of the Holy Spirit. Something that

Satan will always try to do is to stop people from praying, thus rendering them weak and therefore vulnerable. If your knowledge of God does not lead to prayer there is something seriously wrong. The privilege and the power of earnest persistent prayer cannot be stressed too strongly.

Charlotte Elliot gave voice to this in one of her hymns:

> Principalities and powers,
> Mustering their unseen array,
> Wait for your unguarded hours:
> Watch and pray.
>
> Gird your heavenly armour on;
> Wear it ever, night and day;
> Ambushed lies the evil one:
> Watch and pray.

("Watch and Pray," 1839)

Paul says, "keep on praying for all the saints" (v. 18). Every Christian is confronted by the same enemy and so it is vital to pray for each other that the mystery of the gospel will be fearlessly made known. The prayer of all Christian soldiers should not be for comfort or compromise, but for courage to fight the spiritual battle that will ultimately lead to glory.

One day Christ will appear at the head of the heavenly army and complete the victory that He won on the cross. Christians will emerge from the great tribulation and suffer no more. They will join the Church triumphant, a vast crowd too great for any man to count, drawn from every nation, tribe, people and language, standing before God's throne in eternal blessedness. Meanwhile, Christians are to be "salt" and "light" in a corrupt and dark world (Matthew 5:13–16). That can only be achieved by the power of the Holy Spirit.

Summary

The Scriptures speak of spiritual warfare in several places, but it is Paul who addresses the subject most directly in Ephesians 6 where he speaks of the necessity of wearing the full armor of God. This is because our major struggle is not against human beings but against the powers of this dark world (v. 12). The moment you become an active Christian, you become Satan's enemy; the fact that the battle is unseen does not mean that it is not going on. It is vital for us to be constantly aware of the reality of the spiritual battle and to realize that only the power of God can protect us from such a formidable opponent. We need to remember the experience of the Jewish exorcists in Ephesus who foolishly attempted to cast out an evil spirit in the name of Jesus without personally knowing Him. Their attempt was a failure and they fled in panic, naked and badly injured (Acts 19:13–17).

Christians are told to pray specifically for the gift of the Holy Spirit (Luke 11:13; 24:49). God imparted His power to those who prayed at Pentecost, thus fulfilling the prophecies of old. He has not changed and today ordinary people can do extraordinary things by His supernatural power. Prayer should always be our first response rather than our last resort. Scripture and prayer are the two major weapons that the Spirit provides for our defense in spiritual warfare.

To think about and discuss

1. Before the Spirit could come, the Son must go (John 16:7). Why? Is the same power that came upon the apostles at Pentecost available to us today?
2. Why is the whole armor of God essential? What spiritual forces of evil do they protect us against (Ephesians 6:10–17)?

3. Why is prayer essential for defeating the forces of evil? What role does prayer play in my life?
4. Am I living the kind of life that enables me to defend myself against Satan's attacks?

CHAPTER

In Conclusion

7

All Christians belong to the kingdom of heaven to which they have certain obligations. They are to fight for it, not with brutal force but by the power of the Holy Spirit and with love. However, they also live in an earthly kingdom where they must face problems and responsibilities. Jesus said, "You will hear of wars and rumors of wars, but see to it that you are not alarmed. Such things must happen . . . " (Matthew 24:6). Recurring cycles of war are a common characteristic of a fallen world.

The American evangelist Billy Graham commented that if someone was sent from Mars to report earth's major business, "he would in all fairness have to say that its chief industry was war." That is a sad but unexaggerated comment upon humanity. As soon as we remove one tyrant, he or she is replaced by another and so there will always be wars until Christ returns. In the meantime, how should a Christian react to war? Can a Christian be a member of the armed forces or any occupation that might involve injury or death of the opposition? Is it right to have armies for defense? If violence is justified in certain circumstances, are there limits to the means that can be used?

Is it Possible to Justify Nuclear Weapons?

On 6 August 1945 the B29 bomber "Enola Gay" set off on a mission to attack one of three possible targets: Hiroshima, Nagasaki or Kokura. Reconnaissance planes reported clear skies above Hiroshima and so "Little Boy" – the nickname of an atomic bomb – was unleashed at 8.15 a.m. Instantly a kilometer-wide ferocious fireball consumed the city. Three days later the exercise was repeated, this time with a larger bomb on Nagasaki. The final death toll is still unknown but exceeds 100,000 and large areas of both cities were destroyed. Undoubtedly this terrible destruction became a crucial factor in Japan's decision to surrender on 14 August 1945, bringing World War II to an end.

It could be strongly argued that the possession of nuclear weapons enabling retaliation helped maintain peace during the "Cold War." Or that the bombing of Hiroshima and Nagasaki shortened World War II, thus ultimately saving thousands of lives. Does not a strong deterrent promote peace? Despite this argument there are not many today who would defend such action. Would unilateral nuclear disarmament result in aggression? This is debatable but could anything be gained by creating a vast holocaust? Mohamed ElBaradei, the Director General of the International Atomic Energy Agency, when accepting the Nobel Peace Prize in 2005, warned that humanity faces a choice between nuclear weapons and survival. "If we hope to escape self-destruction, I believe nuclear weapons should have no place in our collective conscience and no rule in our security," he said.

Some Christians who are prepared to participate in what they believe to be a just war would consider the possession of nuclear weapons to be immoral. Others would see no moral dilemma inherent in the possession and, if necessary, the use of nuclear weapons for the purpose of retaliatory or revenge strikes. However, such an attitude raises the difficult question of whether it is better to have several decimated populations instead of one. Nuclear warfare would doubtless result in a situation of losers and no winners. Hence, replacing the Trident missile system, which will become obsolete in about 2020, with a new generation of nuclear weaponry at colossal expense would presumably contribute very little to Britain's defense. It also provides an impetus for non-nuclear states to acquire nuclear weapons for their security, thus making the world a more dangerous place.

Can War Ever Be Justified?

Some Christians sincerely believe that they must never engage in physical contact whatever the situation. The Mennonite pacifist Myron S. Augsburger asked, "How can we kill another human being for whom Jesus died? How can we adopt the attitude that 'Jesus loves you, but I'm afraid I'm going to have to kill you'?" The teaching of Jesus in the Sermon on the Mount was:

> "You have heard that it was said, 'Eye for eye, and tooth for tooth.' But I tell you, Do not resist an evil person. If someone strikes you on the right cheek, turn to him the other also."
>
> Matthew 5:38–39)

As we consider these verses we need to remember that "Eye for eye, tooth for tooth" (Exodus 21:24; Leviticus 24:20; Deuteronomy 19:21) was a law of the civil courts laid down in order to prevent offenders from indiscriminate retaliation and excessive punishment. Eye for an eye and not life for an eye avoided such extremes and so spiteful vengeance would be substituted by just retribution. The Pharisees, however, used this law to justify

personal revenge, thus contradicting its very purpose. The
Old Testament clearly and repeatedly forbids such action. For
example:

> "Do not seek revenge or bear a grudge against one of your
> people, but love your neighbor as yourself..."
>
> (Leviticus 19:18)

What does Jesus mean when He says we are to love our
enemies? Surely it tells us not to resist an evil person in a way
that arises from an unloving, unforgiving, revengeful and
vicious disposition. Romans 12:19–21 presents a good illustration of this.

Genuine Wisdom

> ... the wisdom that comes from heaven is first of all pure; then
> peace-loving, considerate, submissive, full of mercy and good
> fruit, impartial and sincere.
>
> (James 3:17)

Heavenly wisdom is pure and it should be observed that purity
is placed before peace. It is always important to make every
effort to live in peace with everyone. Nevertheless, there are
times when both purity and peace together are unattainable:

> If it is possible, as far as it depends on you, live at peace with
> everyone.
>
> (Romans 12:18)

There will unfortunately be situations under which the establishment or maintenance of peace cannot be achieved. "If it is
possible" covers this impossibility.

If the maintenance of peace involves an unacceptable moral compromise, then peace must be abandoned. Lord John Russell rightly said, "If peace cannot be maintained with honor, then it is no longer peace." Or as Geoffrey A. Studdert-Kennedy, an English army chaplain in World War I, once commented, "War is kinder than a Godless peace." To strive for peace at any price is not what the Bible teaches. The major priority must always be purity, whilst the second characteristic of genuine wisdom is to be peace-loving. That is, not only to avoid creating trouble, but actively pursue reconciliation and peace.

The Search for Peace

Many individuals and organizations have attempted to prevent war over the centuries. World War I motivated the creation of the League of Nations in January 1920, with headquarters in Geneva, Switzerland. President Woodrow Wilson of the United States was the chief instigator. He believed that even a powerful nation, knowing that it would face the united opposition of other nations, would be reluctant to go to war. Wilson convinced several countries to agree to his plans for the League – but not the United States' Senate. In March 1920 they rejected the Treaty of Versailles which would have made them a member. Subsequently most Americans were of the opinion that it was unnecessary to concern themselves with conflicts overseas, and so they never joined. Although the League endeavored to provide collective security for its members, it failed to prevent World War II and was formally wound up in April 1946 when its functions were taken over by the United Nations.

The United Nations Security Council consisting of the world's major powers aims to prevent wars or stop them in their infancy. Their first major challenge was the so-called

"Cold War" between the United States and the Soviet Union. Although there was no direct conflict between these two superpowers, their ideological differences caused them to be actively involved in conflicts elsewhere. At this time the arms race resulted in colossal stockpiles of weapons and nuclear disaster was a distinct possibility. President John F. Kennedy, speaking to the United Nations General Assembly in September 1961, said, "Every man, woman and child lives under a nuclear sword of Damocles, hanging by the slenderest of threads, capable of being cut at any moment by accident, miscalculation or madness."

Despite the efforts of the United Nations there have been many international conflicts and civil disturbances since World War II. Even so, irrespective of these failings, anything that helps to prevent unjust conflict should be encouraged. All Christians should make every effort to live in peace with all men (Hebrews 12:14). Jesus said:

"Blessed are the peacemakers,
　　for they will be called sons of God."

(Matthew 5:9)

This is probably one of the most popular of all the Beatitudes and will meet with almost universal approval regardless of whether one is a Christian or not. Only the extreme militant could object to peacemaking.

Governments are subject to the sovereignty of God (Daniel 2:21; 4:17, 31). They are appointed by Him and have a responsibility to punish those who do wrong and praise those who do right (Romans 13; 1 Peter 2). Consequently, the responsibility of all citizens is to submit to the authority of their government providing that it does not involve violating any of God's commands.

As we saw in chapter 3, there are, however, certain circum-stances when it is permissible and even mandatory for a Christian to participate in acts of civil disobedience and the Bible provides us with a number of precedents: for example, if a government were to pass a law forbidding Christians from proclaiming the gospel message. When this problem was encountered by the early Church, they rightly refused to obey (Acts 4:18–20; 5:18–21, 40–42). However, it would have been wrong for them to preach in places where they were strongly opposed, thus deliberately causing civil unrest (Matthew 10:11–16, 23).

Sometimes the issues are not so clear cut and Christians are divided about the rights and wrongs of civil disobedience. Consider abortion, for example. Some Christians believe that, because of such texts as Proverbs 24:11, action is mandatory. Others claim that active disobedience is unnecessary since the law does not demand or require that you agree with abortion. Nor is there anything to prevent the individual from peacefully attempting to change the law to make abortion illegal.

The establishment of guiding criteria can be very useful in this difficult area of civil disobedience. Obviously it must always be contrary to the Word of God to resist the law. Acts of civil disobedience should only be undertaken after all legal means of changing an unjust situation have been exhausted. As with war, it should always be a last resort and those who participate must be willing to accept the penalty whatever the cost. Finally, as far as it depends on any Christian involved, all action must be non-violent.

Should Christians Join the Armed Forces?

Christians who volunteer to serve in the armed forces always need to remember that they are required to swear obedience to a civil or military authority. They must also realize the possibility of being called upon to kill innocent civilians deliberately. It would be a serious mistake to believe otherwise for no government is immune to committing atrocities, not even a British or American one.

On the night of 13 February 1945, the beautiful German city of Dresden experienced horrendous and unnecessary destruction. British and American forces were responsible for a savage saturation bombing that reduced the city to a smoldering heap of ruins. Thousands of innocent people who were themselves victims of Nazism were killed.

Roy Akehurst, a wireless operator who took part in the raid on Dresden, said, "It struck me at the time, the thought of the women and children down there. We seemed to fly for hours over a sheet of fire – a terrific red glow with thin haze over it. I found myself making comments to the crew: Oh God, those poor people. It was completely uncalled for. You can't justify it." Anyone who joins the armed forces needs to ask themselves how they would react if they were ordered to attack civilian targets indiscriminately. Would they be able to obey orders knowing that they were immoral? Anyone who decides upon a military career must do so with a good conscience and only after much careful thought and prayer.

Christians should also consider the question of whether they should aim for positions of responsibility and leadership in all aspects of life, so that they are able to influence others and make things happen – or prevent things from happening. Ambition for power can affect people in many ways. They may strive for personal position and glorification, or they may be motivated by the desire to benefit others and glorify God.

Contrary to a widely held view the New Testament does not teach complete pacifism: it was church fathers such as Tertullian, Origen and Cyprian who promoted this position. Neither Jesus nor the apostles ever told soldiers to quit the military and it is interesting to note that the first Gentile convert to Christianity was a Roman centurion (Acts 10). He was not condemned because of his profession but commended by the Lord for his faith.

A Christian's life is never easy; it is a battle against the unseen and powerful forces of evil, as we saw in chapter 6 which examined the vital issue of spiritual warfare. As long as sin exists in the world, Christians must constantly be aware of their complete dependence upon the inexhaustible power of God. Physical and spiritual wars will continue until the final great battle when Jesus Christ will be the victor. Then the world as we know it will be brought to an end.

A Time When War Will Cease

God promises that one day all war will cease.

> "He will judge between the nations
> and will settle disputes for many peoples.
> They will beat their swords into plowshares
> and their spears into pruning hooks.
> Nation will not take up sword against nation,
> nor will they train for war anymore."
>
> (Isaiah 2:4)

Weapons of destruction will be refashioned into implements of peace and prosperity. Individuals will no longer fight each other as in Genesis 4, or nation fight nation as in Genesis 14. When the hearts of men have been regenerated by the Spirit of God it will result in universal peace.

In words which although used in a different context are almost identical to those of Isaiah, Micah makes the same promise (Micah 4:3). This raises the question of whether Micah quoted Isaiah, or vice versa, or whether they both quoted from an earlier anonymous prophet. Despite much intellectual speculation it is impossible to say with any certainty, but whatever the answer it does not detract from the importance of these prophecies.

As I mentioned earlier, there are occasions in the Bible when verses appear to contradict each other, and this is one of them. Compare the words of the prophet Joel,

> "Beat your plowshares into swords
>   and your pruning hooks into spears . . . "

(Joel 3:10)

Although seemingly at odds with the character of the kingdom of God, his exhortation is not in fact contradictory to the overall Bible message. In this instance Joel was calling the nations to prepare for holy war. "Holy" because it is instigated by the Lord Himself to confirm His holiness.

Isaiah and Micah, on the other hand, were referring to a different period in human history, namely the period of God's future reign on earth. At that time, Micah goes on to tell us:

> "Every man will sit under his own vine
>   and under his own fig-tree,
> and no-one will make them afraid,
>   for the Lord Almighty has spoken."

(Micah 4:4)

These promises look to the future. While in a spiritual sense the peace of God, which transcends all understanding, guarding our hearts and minds in Christ Jesus, can be experienced now (Philippians 4:7), the Bible tells us that the best is yet to come.

There will be a day when peace and tranquility are universal, symbolized in the beautiful picture that, "Every man will sit under his own vine and under his own fig-tree" (cf. 1 Kings 4:24b–25; Zechariah 3:10). In that day there will no longer be any need to be afraid. This time will surely come, because the Lord Almighty has declared the certainty of the fulfillment of His promise.

The Return of Christ

The Book of Revelation reveals an awesome picture of the emergence of the conquering Christ (19:11–21). He is no longer gentle and riding on a donkey of peace (Zechariah 9:9; Matthew 21:5), but coming from heaven on a white horse of war. This creates many problems for those who believe that Jesus was always a pacifist, despite His declaration to the contrary:

> "Do not suppose that I have come to bring peace to the earth. I did not come to bring peace, but a sword."
>
> (Matthew 10:34; Luke 12:51)

Although some try to "spiritualize" these words of Christ, it is more difficult to do so after reading Revelation where the obvious interpretation of the final conflict is physical. Only by ignoring part of the teaching of the New Testament could you ever reach the conclusion that Christ is never a military figure. In the final scenes of world history He is clearly depicted by John as the heavenly warrior-king, with the vast armies of heaven following Him. "He is dressed in a robe dipped in blood" (19:13), not His own but that of His enemies.

> Out of his mouth comes a sharp sword with which to strike down the nations. "He will rule them with an iron scepter."

> He treads the winepress of the fury of the wrath of God
> Almighty.
>
> (v. 15)

This sword is not the comforting word of the gospel but the
sword of judgment with which He strikes down the nations.
Jesus' rule with an iron scepter fulfils Isaiah's prophecy that:

> He will strike the earth with the rod of his mouth;
>   with the breath of his lips he will slay the wicked.
>
> (Isaiah 11:4)

The treading of the winepress is a sign of severe judgment
(Isaiah 63:1–6; Joel 3:12–14).

The picture portrayed of Jesus in Revelation is not the
"Gentle Jesus, meek and mild" that we sing of in the well-
known hymn written by Charles Wesley. Why not? Has Jesus
changed since He first came to earth? No, it is the purpose of
His mission that is different. His first visit was to seek and to
save what was lost (Luke 19:10). He came as a Savior not as a
Judge. But when He returns, the position will be reversed. Jesus
is then depicted as leading a mass slaughter: the slaughter of
Armageddon.

Some mystery surrounds the Hebrew name *Har-Magedon* (in
Greek, *Armageddon*), which means "Mount of Megiddo." The
exact geographical location of this mount has not been
identified, though an ancient city called Megiddo existed in
the western part of the Plain of Esdraelon. Megiddo was on a
junction of major international trade routes and also guarded
the northern entrance to Israel. Because of its strategic
importance in the protection of Israel and Judah, many decisive
battles were fought here in biblical times. It was at Megiddo
that Deborah and Barak defeated the Canaanites who, under

their king Jabin and his general Sisera (Judges 4), had been opposing the Israelites and that King Ahaziah died (2 Kings 9:27). It was also at Megiddo that King Josiah was slain whilst in battle with Pharaoh Neco (2 Kings 23:29). Historically this was an important battle in that it delayed Neco in his attempt to reach Haran and aid Assyria against Babylon. Consequently, the Assyrian army were defeated and Babylon became the leading power of the east.

Although Armageddon is named only once in the Bible (Revelation 16:16) it is the well-known designation for the final great battle between the forces of good and evil (Revelation 19:11–21). Some would argue that this does not refer to a military battle between human armies that will be fought at some future date, but rather is used symbolically to describe a spiritual battle between the army of Satan and the forces of God. What is certain is that this battle will be fought and all evil powers will be defeated.

The last judgment (Revelation 20:11–15) is the day that God has chosen "when he will judge the world with justice by the man he has appointed. He has given proof of this to all men by raising him from the dead" (Acts 17:31). Everyone who has ever lived will be judged by the Lord Jesus Christ and so there will be no fear of any miscarriage of justice. Each of us will be judged according to our actions and all will be revealed. Does this suggest that you can be acceptable in God's sight because of good works? The answer is no, for "Another book was opened, which is the book of life" (Revelation 20:12). In chapter 21 verse 27 it is called "the Lamb's book of life" which contains the names of all who have been reconciled with God. Therefore, Christians need not fear the judgment for Christ was judged in their place, the just for the unjust.

The final two chapters of the Book of Revelation turn from the destruction of God's enemies to a new heaven and a new earth. Wars, diseases and all destructive forces will cease. Those who are acceptable to God will live forever in His presence; man finally re-enters the Paradise from which since Adam's fall he has been estranged (Genesis 3:23). Meanwhile Christians are to live at peace whenever possible. Blessed are the rational for they will carefully consider all of God's Word prior to reaching their decision.

Each of the events that have been considered should be a warning of the necessity to flee the coming wrath. They are also a reminder and an encouragement to all believers that God will protect those who have committed themselves to Him. Our concern should be to prepare for that day and to proclaim the good news about Jesus.

The grace of the Lord Jesus be with God's people. Amen.

(Revelation 22:21)

Summary

It is a fact that following careful and prayerful consideration Christians may disagree. Some will be pacifists; others will differ in what they consider to be a just or unjust war. There are those who will consider it to have been acceptable to fight in World War II, but have doubts or serious conscientious objections to the invasion of Iraq in 2003. How should Christians react to war? Based on my studies, a strict pacifist position appears to be unbiblical. The fact that we live in a sinful world means that it is sometimes regrettably necessary to go to war. However, the legitimacy of any war must be very carefully evaluated before taking action. This conviction will be at variance with some of my fellow Christians, but I trust that they will respect my views even though they cannot share them.

Christians must act according to their conscience and always do what they sincerely believe to be right. Conflict should be avoided whenever possible, because this always arises when opposing viewpoints are unwilling to find common ground. Therefore, when Christians disagree it is useful for them to remember what they have in common. They worship the same God, are possessed by the same Spirit, attacked by the same devil, and by grace and through faith in Jesus Christ are destined to experience the same glory. Apart from these truths Christians may have little in common. They differ from one another in culture, education, personality, temperament and in many other ways. Thank God we do. It should not prevent fellowship because Christians differ on issues relating to pacifism or war. There are much more important issues than peace and war. The fact that war exists is indicative that we live in a sinful world. Ever since Adam and Eve the world has been in a war between good and evil. Therefore, our first priority must be to guard our own conduct and proclaim that all who call on the name of the Lord will be saved.

To think about and discuss

1. Selwyn Hughes says, "It has always amazed me how Christians can write the most bitter things and then sign their letters 'Yours in Christ'! I would have thought that being 'in Christ' meant having His mindset in all things" (*My Story*, CWR, 2004, p. 357). Occasionally those who consider themselves to be pacifists can become extremely militant when discussing such a controversial subject as war. Why? How can Christians avoid bitterness towards each other?

2. Compare Joel 3:10 with Isaiah 2:4. How do you explain the apparent contradiction?

3. God is a God of love and a God of wrath. Why is it
    dangerous to place undue emphasis upon a particular
    attribute of God?
4. "Whoever believes in the Son has eternal life, but
    whoever rejects the Son will not see life, for God's
    wrath remains on him" (John 3:36). What is your
    response to Christ's invitation?

We hope you enjoyed reading this Sovereign World book.
For more details of other Sovereign books and
new releases see our website:

www.sovereignworld.com

If you would like to help us send a copy of this book
and many other titles to needy pastors in developing
countries, please write for further information
or send your gift to:

Sovereign World Trust
PO Box 777
Tonbridge, Kent TN11 0ZS
United Kingdom

You can also visit **www.sovereignworldtrust.com**.
The Trust is a registered charity.